felt furnishings

ANNE KYYRÖ QUINN

felt furnishings

25 ACCESSORIES FOR CONTEMPORARY HOMES

photography by CHRIS EVERARD

POTTER
CRAFT
New York

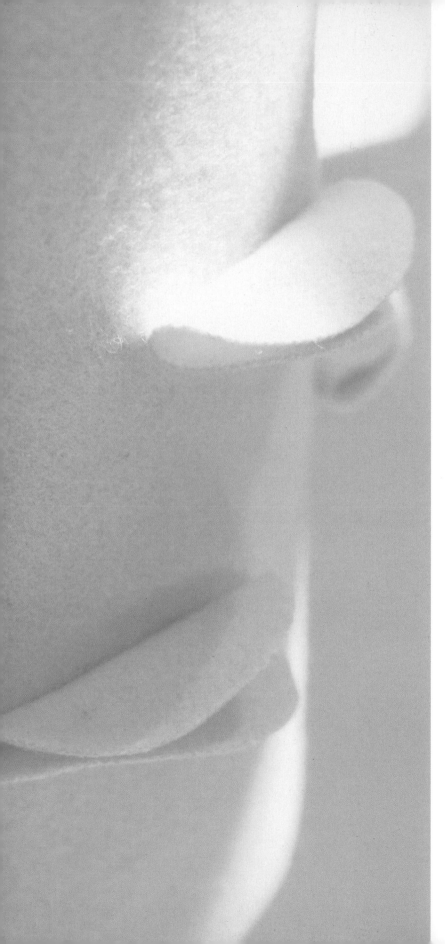

Published in the United States by Potter Craft, an imprint of the
Crown Publishing Group, a division of Random House, Inc., New York.
www.crownpublishing.com
www.pottercraft.com

POTTER CRAFT and colophon is a registered trademark of
Random House, Inc.

Originally published in the United Kingdom by Jacqui Small LLP,
an imprint of Aurum Press Ltd, London.

Library of Congress Cataloging-in-Publication Data is available
upon request.

ISBN: 978-0-307-45151-4

Printed in China

10 9 8 7 6 5 4 3 2 1

First American Edition

PUBLISHER Jacqui Small
ART DIRECTOR Valerie Fong
COMMISSIONING EDITOR Zia Mattocks
PRODUCTION Peter Colley

To my tutors, mentors, and friends – Paula Ashbrooke and Terry Bullent

CONTENTS

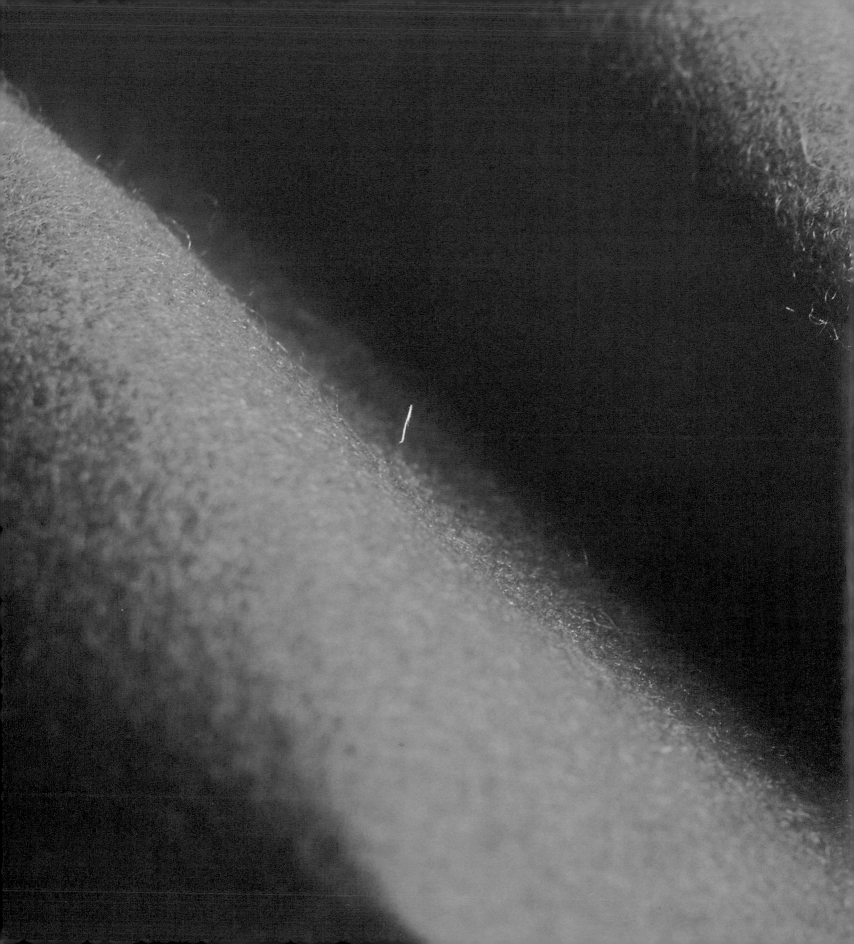

introduction

introduction

AS FAR BACK AS I CAN REMEMBER, I HAVE ALWAYS LOVED MAKING THINGS, AND EVEN AS A VERY SMALL CHILD I WAS DRAWN TO ARTS AND CRAFTS. WHEN MY MOTHER MOVED RECENTLY, I FOUND SOME OF THE THINGS I HAD CREATED AS A CHILD, AND IT WAS INTERESTING TO SEE THAT MANY OF THEM WERE CRAFTED IN FELT.

Since my childhood experiments, I didn't rediscover felt until my final year studying Textile Design at London Metropolitan University, where my tutor, Paula Ashbrooke, encouraged me to use felt as part of my final project. It is an exciting material to work with and I could see endless possibilities for using it in innovative ways. Since then, I have dedicated my career as

a textile designer to discovering and developing new techniques to manipulate wool felts. For the past ten years I have been applying felt in various ways to create different projects and products. My work has included several collections of felt home furnishings, spanning lighting, pillows, throws, table textiles, window treatments, and wall hangings.

Initially, I worked with handmade felt. I experimented with lots of types of wool, discovering how different quality wools from different breeds of sheep felt in distinctive ways. I also experimented with various techniques, finding out how to control the density and thickness of the fabric by felting, boiling, and shrinking the wool. When handmaking felt, the wet wool is very malleable, so it can be easily formed into three-dimensional shapes. It is also possible to create seamless structures, which are often used for hats and other molded products.

If you have not made felt yourself, I urge you to try it and to experiment as I did (there are many good classes, and felt-making kits are readily available from craft suppliers). There is something very satisfying and rewarding about the whole process—from selecting the types of wool, to carding (combing and brushing the wool), and then manipulating it in the hot, soapy water. I became so fascinated by the process that I even spent time varying the amount and type of soap, and altering all the other variables to see the different effects that this produced. As a result, my felt experiments became very sculptural and my signature multi-dimensional surface structures were born. I then started working with industrially produced felts and heavy felted woven-wool fabrics, re-creating the designs I had formed using handmade felt, and I found these fabrics to be very versatile and adaptable.

What is felt?

Felt is a nonwoven cloth that is produced by the matting, condensing, and pressing together of fibers, commonly animal fur or wool. Traditional handmade felt is created by rubbing woolen fleece in a small amount of water (preferably hot and soapy). This makes the wool fibers interlock and become denser; when cooled, dried, and compressed, the scales of the fibers close and lock. Handmade felt has been used throughout history for various purposes, including clothing, rugs, and tents. There are some who maintain that certain types of animal or breeds produce the best felt; that sheep reared in hot countries will produce fleeces with tighter curls, which in turn will produce a better bond and so result in denser fabric. If you are felting by hand and looking to achieve a certain finish, these may be considerations, but for the purpose of this book, any standard wool felt will be ideal.

> Felt is an exciting material to work with. It can be manipulated by various methods to create different effects, and there are endless possibilities for using it in innovative ways.

It is possible to buy felt made from many different fibers, and indeed mixtures of fibers, but I recommend using 100 percent wool felt, which is highly absorbent, soft, and warm. There are a number of synthetic felts and needlepoint felts available, but these have usually been developed for a specific purpose, such as insulation or carpet underlay, and are generally not suitable for the projects in this book. Synthetic felts tend to pill.

Wool is also, of course, a natural and renewable resource, making it an appealing choice of material. Other advantages are that wool has a tendency to absorb water, but it is slow to feel damp. Its ability to absorb moisture adds to its natural fire-retardancy and allows for ease

opposite For this table runner, two long strips of felt in different colors have been sewn together, and the simple leaf-shaped design has been cut out of the top layer to reveal the contrasting color underneath. The cutout shapes were then used as appliqués to make the matching place mats.

of dyeing. Wool felt shares some of these basic qualities—the absorbency has long been exploited for wicks, and even refined into felt-tipped pens. In addition, specialized felts are often used in industries such as printing, where they help to lubricate the presses, squeezing out a small amount of oil with every movement. In my native Finland, we wear felt boots in winter, as they are exceptionally warm, and the dense meshing of the fibers makes them effectively waterproof, which is essential when walking through the snow. Wool felt is an amazing material, with a number of special qualities that make it different from other fabrics:

∗ Wool felt is a very hardwearing cloth, making it particularly well suited for a number of uses in the home.

∗ Felt does not fray, so the cut edges do not require finishing; this makes it ideal for appliqué.

∗ Felt comes in various thicknesses and densities—it can be made hard enough to be used as an industrial polishing tool, or it can be soft and flexible enough to sew.

∗ Felt has excellent insulating properties, so it is well suited for making wall hangings and blinds, as well as place mats.

∗ Felt absorbs sound and vibration—it is extensively used in heavy industries for this reason.

> In addition to being a natural and renewable resource, wool is soft, warm, and insulating. Wool felt shares these properties and is also hardwearing as well as fire-retardant.

Felted woven-wool fabric

In addition to pressed felt, I have used felted, tightly-woven woolen fabric for some of the projects. "Woven felt" is a confusing oxymoron, as by definition felt is not woven. To add to the confusion, "woven felt" is often referred to simply as "felt" in some countries. Although it is created by a different method, it has many of the same qualities of true felt—it does not really fray and has a very pronounced nap that mimics felt. Felted woven-wool fabric is usually available in a wider range of colors than pressed felt.

Boiled wool is another term sometimes used for this sort of material, but specifically refers to knitted wool. Anyone who has ever attempted to wash a woolen sweater in hot water knows that the results can be traumatic, as there is a tendency for the garment to shrink and harden—in other words to "felt"—as the fibers mat even closer together.

below Appliqué is a very simple way to add colorful surface decoration to anything from a pillow cover to a throw. It is a technique that has been used to decorate felt textiles for centuries.

Similarly, interesting effects can be achieved by machine-washing felt on a hot cycle. I would normally recommend that felt products are only subjected to specialist dry cleaning, but I have spent long periods of time testing how felts of various thicknesses react to different machine washes and temperatures. The effects can be quite striking, as the felt can start to unravel, giving it a softer, fuzzier look. I would recommend that when experimenting with this process, always try a small sample first. Once you have decided on the right look for your project and determined the temperature needed to achieve it, another variable is whether you wash the felt before or after sewing it up, as the stitching threads will shrink at a

different rate than the felt. This can create interesting effects with a number of the techniques used in this book, but I have not discussed the options within each project instructions, as the result will vary dramatically depending on the quality of the fabric used and the individual washing-machine programs.

The collection of designs

The 25 projects I have included in this book are designed to suit all sewing abilities, and range from very simple to more technically challenging. The method for each project is explained in simple steps, and I have also suggested variations and alternative ideas for some of the projects to encourage experimentation with felt fabrics. Commonly known soft-furnishing techniques have been used, such as ruching, gathering, pleating, appliqué, and freehand machine embroidery, all of which can be easily carried out using a basic home sewing machine.

The materials required are usually readily available from well-stocked fabric and craft suppliers, and felt can also be ordered online from various websites (see the Resources on page 142). Felt and felted wool fabric comes in many different widths, so I recommend reading the instructions before you shop, as you may need to buy larger amounts of a narrower felt than specified and join pieces together. Most of the projects could also be created from recycled woolen items, such as sweaters and blankets, by "boiling" them in a hot machine wash to shrink and harden the fabric before turning it into felt furnishings.

The projects have been divided into four chapters according to the techniques used—Gathers + Ruches, Pleats + Folds, Appliqués + Cutouts, and Strips + Slices. Each chapter offers a wide variety of home-furnishing projects, ranging from place mats to bedspreads, from pillows to curtains. However, the techniques introduced are mostly ways to manipulate the surface of the textiles, so they are interchangeable and can be applied to many different projects and items.

> The techniques used throughout are mostly ways to manipulate the surface of the textiles, so they are interchangeable and can be applied to many different projects.

The first chapter introduces simple gathering and ruching. These are techniques not usually associated with heavy fabrics like felt or felted woven wool, but are used more commonly for soft furnishings made of lighter materials, such as chintz and silks.

The use of various pleating techniques is illustrated in the second chapter. These include knife pleats, box pleats, tubular pleats, and simple tucking techniques, where small pleats are stitched along their entire length.

The third chapter introduces basic machine appliqué. Unlike most of the other techniques used throughout the book, the resulting surface structure is relatively flat.

In the fourth chapter, I have used cut and torn ribbons of felt to create soft furnishings with crisp simple lines and a modern feel. Experimenting with machine-washing the felt would, perhaps, produce the most interesting results with the projects in this chapter. This is also the best section in which to use scraps of felt and felted recycled wool.

The final section describes the basic sewing equipment needed for the projects. It also includes two easy ways to make up pillow backs and shows how to create some simple felt decorations that can be used to embellish any of the projects in this book. Lastly, there are templates for four of the projects and a useful list of suppliers of materials and equipment.

gathers + ruches

gathers + ruches

SOMETIMES AN IDEA FOR A NEW DESIGN WILL COME TO ME WHEN I'M PLAYING AROUND WITH A PIECE OF FELT IN MY HAND. I OFTEN FIND THAT, WHEN I'M TWISTING AND MANIPULATING THE CLOTH, IT STARTS TO SUGGEST INTERESTING FORMS AND SHAPES THAT COULD BE USED AS DECORATIVE SCULPTURAL SURFACE TREATMENTS.

To capture these forms, in this chapter I have used the traditional techniques of gathering and ruching to create highly textural surface structures from felt and felted wool fabric. Some of these techniques are perhaps more often associated with floral-patterned chintz and lavishly deployed in extravagant soft furnishings; however, when using natural felt or heavy woolen cloth, these same techniques can create a totally different look that is modern, sculptural, and organic. To help to update these techniques even more, I have carefully balanced the flat and raised surface areas within my designs to create a distinct contrast between the textured, frilled, or ruched cloth and the areas of smooth, single-colored felt or wool fabric.

The matte surface and heavy weight of felt or felted wool fabrics gives traditional gathers, ruches, and frills a totally different look that is modern, sculptural, and organic.

As the cloth used is heavy and thick, when making a gathered frill, it is important to choose a strong thread to use for the gathering thread. It is essential that care is taken when gathering the frill, to ensure that the frill appears as evenly gathered as possible. When positioning the frilled fabric on the base fabric, pin or tack it in place to make sure that it will not move around when the fabrics are machine-sewn together.

For the Decorative Pillow with Spiral Rosette (see pages 18–21), I have used ripped strips of felted, tightly-woven woolen cloth because ripping instead of cutting the cloth makes the edges appear soft and fluffy. When positioning the gathered frill on the base fabric in the spiral design, it is important to follow the marked guidelines carefully so that you build up an even pattern. The rows of frills should be placed very close to one another, in order to maximize the fullness of the textured look. The same applies to

below Strips of felted wool, which have been ripped rather than cut to create soft, fluffy edges, have been joined end to end and then gathered along one long edge to create a frill. This has been sewn onto a pillow cover in a tight spiral design, so that the frills overlap and create a raised surface.

the rosette clusters used on pages 34–37, which have been sewn onto the surface of the pillow very close to one another, to form a dense three-dimensional surface.

Festoon blinds are based entirely on the concept of gathered fabric. In recent years, traditional ruched blinds have been considered somewhat old-fashioned and fussy for modern interiors. Reinterpreted in felt, however, the Festoon Blind takes on an unexpectedly contemporary feel, and the play of light and shadow on the gathers of this understated matte cloth adds a distinctive textural interest to an otherwise clean-lined interior (see pages 26–29).

The petals that make up the Bold Flower Pillow (see pages 30–33) are gathered individually at one end; the gathered ends are then attached around a circle drawn in the middle of the base panel. For the best result, make sure that all five petals are gathered evenly before being spaced carefully around the edge of the circle to create the effect of a flower center in the middle of the pillow. The other ends of the petals are simply boxpleated, then tucked into the side seams of the pillow before they are sewn together. The sheer volume of the fabric used for the gathered petals creates a soft, raised effect—you can either reduce this by making the petals a little shorter before boxpleating them, or add extra fullness by placing polyester batting under the petals to pad them out.

When choosing the colors to use for your gathered and ruched projects, bear in mind that tonal shades will enhance the play of light and shadow, while a contrasting color could be used for the gathered areas to further emphasize the effect of the textured detail against the flat background. Patterned fabric could also be used for the gathered detail, which would create an interesting effect, as the pattern would distort and make the colors merge.

decorative pillow with **spiral rosette**

For this pillow cover I used a variation on the classic rosette. To emphasize the contrast between the textured detailing of the flower motif and the smooth background surface, I have layered the coils of the fabric strip very close to one another so that they stand up—wider spacing between the coils will create a flatter effect. To achieve a softer, more organic look, I used a felted wool fabric that is easy to tear, creating the soft frayed edges. Pressed felt does not tear easily, but it could be used instead and cut into strips to give a sharper, crisper finish.

previous page Using fabric in the same color for both the decorative motif and the background of this pillow cover has at once simplified and updated the traditional rosette, expressing the three-dimensional nature of the design in a subtle, understated way.

1 If you wish to make a pillow back with a zipper, cut three pieces of fabric for the pillow cover—one for the front measuring 25 x25" (62 x 62cm) and two for the back measuring 25 x 13½" (62 x 33cm) and 25 x 13" (62 x 32cm). If you wish to make a sewn-in pillow back, cut the back panel to the same measurements as the front.

For the spiral rosette, rip the fabric into ten 2½"- (6cm-) wide pieces to create a frayed edge.

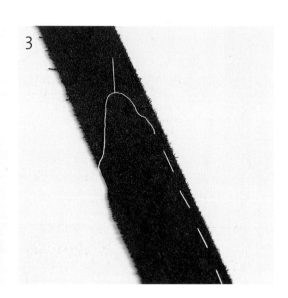

materials + tools
FEATHER PILLOW INSERT, 24 x 24"
   (60 x 60CM)
FOR THE PILLOW COVER: 25 x 52"
   (62 x 127CM) DARK GRAY FELTED
   WOVEN-WOOL FABRIC
FOR THE SPIRAL ROSETTE: 24 x 56"
   (60 x 140CM) DARK GRAY FELTED
   WOVEN-WOOL FABRIC
MATCHING ZIPPER, 24" (60CM) LONG
   (OPTIONAL—SEE PAGES 126–127)
MATCHING SEWING THREAD
BASIC SEWING KIT
SEWING MACHINE

2 Join the ten strips together end to end to form one continuous long strip for the spiral rosette. Pin, then machine-sew the ends together using straight stitch, approximately ¼" (5mm) from the edge. (Contrasting stitching has been used so that it shows up in the photograph, but use matching dark gray sewing thread.)

3 To create a frilled edge, hand-sew a gathering stitch ¼" (5mm) from one edge of the strip all the way along its length. (Again, use matching sewing thread instead of contrasting thread.)

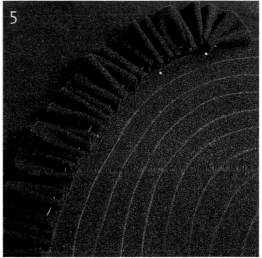

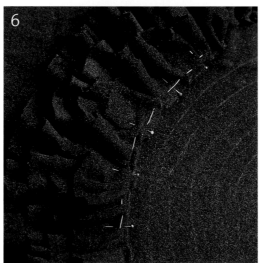

4 Holding the gathering thread with one hand and the end of the fabric strip with the other, gently pull the thread and push the fabric strip along it to form a random and irregular frill.

5 Using tailor's chalk, draw a circle with a 20" (50cm) diameter in the center of the front pillow panel. Draw ever-decreasing circles inside the first, spacing them ¾" (2cm) apart. Align the gathered edge of the strip along the outer circle with the frill facing outward, and start pinning in place.

6 Continue pinning the gathered strip all the way around the outer circle until you reach your starting point, then ease the strip onto the next circle, working inward toward the center of the pillow and leaving a ¾" (2cm) gap between layers.

7 Machine-sew the frilled strip in place, stitching approximately ¼" (5mm) from the edge of the strip and holding back the adjacent layer as you work. Remove the gathering thread.
Make up the pillow back and join the front and back as described on page 126 or 127. Insert the pillow form into the finished cover.

Decorative pillows used in pairs or groups add a welcoming feel to an interior and can be used to introduce an accent color to a neutral scheme. Here, a chic monochrome look has been achieved with two bold red pillows on a cream sofa. Variations in shape, size, and design can help to create pace, so a large square pillow with a vertical gathered seam (see right for instructions) has been paired with a smaller rectangular pillow with a horizontal gathered seam.

gathered-seam pillow

Depending on the desired effect, you can adapt the seam detail
in a number of ways. You may wish to sew more or fewer lines of
machine stitching, in either a matching or contrasting color, or
you can gather the seam more to increase the ruching on the front
of the pillow—if you do this, allow more fabric width accordingly.
Our measurements correspond to the larger square pillow.

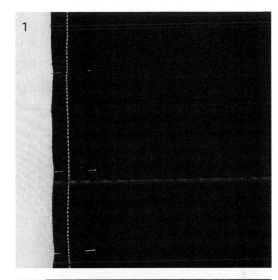

materials + tools
FEATHER PILLOW INSERT, 24 x 24" (60 x 60CM)
32 x 62" (80 x 156CM) RED FELT OR FELTED
   WOVEN-WOOL FABRIC
MATCHING OR CONTRASTING SEWING THREAD
BASIC SEWING KIT
SEWING MACHINE

1 Cut two pieces of fabric measuring 32 x 13½"
(80 x 34cm) for the front of the pillow cover. Cut
two more pieces of fabric measuring 25 x 17½"
(63 x 44cm) for the back of the cover and set aside.
With wrong sides facing, pin the first two pieces
of fabric together along the 32" (80cm) edge,
then machine-sew ¼" (5mm) in from the edge.

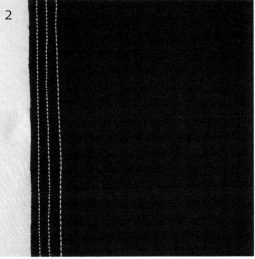

2 Machine-sew three more parallel lines
alongside the seam, leaving a ¼" (5mm) gap
between each row of stitching.

3 Open up the fabric so that the seam is in
the center, facing up—this is the right side of the
pillow cover. Hand-sew two separate lines of
running stitch, one on each side of the central
seam, working parallel to the lines of machine
stitching and ¼" (5mm) away from the last line.
Leave a long tail of thread at the beginning
and end of each line of running stitch, and
ensure that you start and finish on the right side
of the fabric. When you have finished, knot the
threads together at each end.

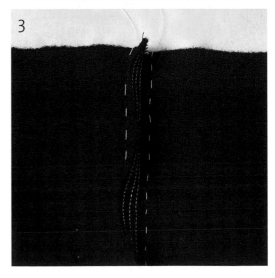

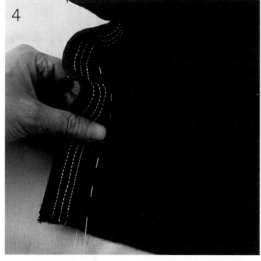

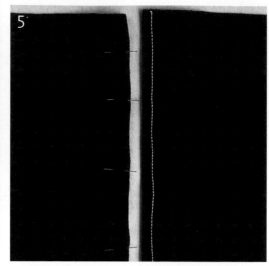

opposite A gathered seam creates lovely irregular soft folds in the fabric on either side of it. Different effects can be achieved by gathering the seam more or less tightly. You can also vary the stitch detail on the seam by sewing more or fewer lines of machine stitching in matching or contrasting thread, or using straight or zigzag stitch.

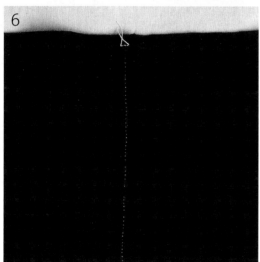

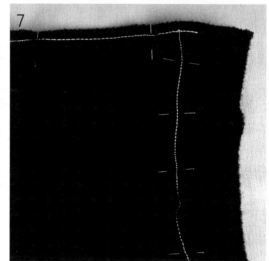

4 Hold the knotted threads at one end, and gently pull the fabric and thread away from each other to create a ruched effect, being careful not to break the threads. Ease the fabric along the thread, working toward the middle, then start gathering the fabric from the other end until the ruched seam measures 25" (63cm). Knot the threads and secure with a few stitches at each end.

5 To make up the back of the pillow, take the two remaining pieces of fabric and pin a ¾" (2cm) hem along one 25" (63cm) edge of each piece. Topstitch the hems to create neat edges for the overlapping back panels of the pillow cover.

6 With the hems in the center, right side up, overlap the two back pieces by about 4¼" (10.5cm) to form a 25" (63cm) square; secure temporarily with a couple of stitches at the top and bottom.

7 With right sides together, center the front piece on the back piece—because of the gathered seam, there will be an overlap of fabric that can be cut away after sewing. Using a ½" (1.5cm) seam allowance, pin across the gathering in a straight line, then pin the other sides together to create a 24" (60cm) square. Machine-sew along all four seams, then trim away the excess fabric. Turn the cover right sides out, and insert the pillow form.

festoon blind

Not often associated with modern interior style, a festoon blind such as this is an excellent way of adding texture to a room. The blind creates billowing folds of ruched fabric when it is drawn up, and retains a gentle undulating quality when it is fully extended over the window. On a practical level, the thick cloth is insulating and blocks out light effectively. This blind is quite tightly gathered, but you can vary the tightness of the folds to create a less dramatic effect.

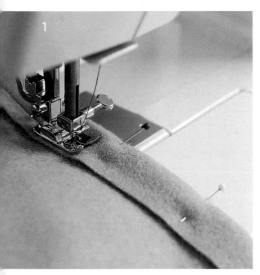 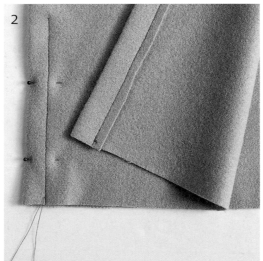 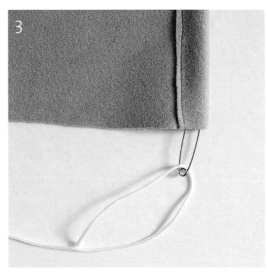

materials + tools

BLUE FELT OR FELTED WOVEN-WOOL
    FABRIC (SEE STEP 1 FOR QUANTITY)
NYLON CORD TO GATHER THE BLIND AND
    TO LIFT IT (SEE STEP 1 FOR LENGTHS)
WOODEN BATTEN (WIDTH OF WINDOW)
HOOK-AND-EYE TAPE, AS ABOVE
9 PLASTIC OR METAL CURTAIN RINGS,
    ½" (1CM) DIAMETER
3 SCREW EYES, ½" (1CM) DIAMETER,
    1" (2.5CM) LONG
1 CLEAT, ¾ X ⅝" (2 X 1.5CM)
MATCHING SEWING THREAD
BASIC SEWING KIT & SEWING MACHINE
STAPLE GUN & STAPLES

1 Measure the window and calculate its width plus 3½" (9cm) for the three gathering channels, and 2.5 times its length from the top of the frame to the sill. Cut a piece of fabric to these measurements. Set aside another piece of fabric large enough to cover the wooden batten.

For the gathering cords, which create the ruching, cut three strands of strong nylon cord to the same length as the main piece of fabric plus an extra 8" (20cm). For the lifting cords, which raise and lower the blind, cut three more strands of nylon cord to 2.5 times the length of the window.

To form the side channels for the gathering cords, fold both side edges over by 1" (2.5cm), and

pin in place on the back of the blind. Machine-sew along the length, sewing ¾" (2cm) in from the folded edge. Repeat on the other side.

2 To form the center channel, mark the center point of the fabric with a pin at the top and bottom; with wrong sides together, fold the fabric in half along this length, and pin in place. Machine-sew the channel ¾" (2cm) in from the fold.

3 Using a safety pin attached to one end of the nylon gathering cord, feed each length of cord through the three channels. Leave approximately 4" (10cm) of excess cord at each end of the blind.

previous page When it is ruched, the felted wool looks both soft and structured, and there is an interesting play of light and shadow on the folds of the fabric, which combine to bring a unique decorative effect to the room.

4 Before gathering the cords to ruche the fabric, secure them to the bottom end of the blind by machine-sewing ⅜" (1cm) in from the bottom of each channel over the cord. Trim the excess cord.

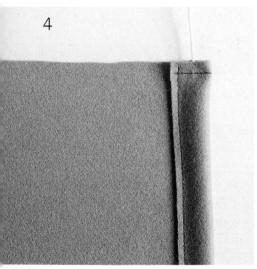

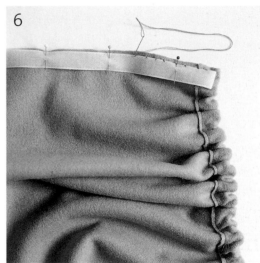

5 To gather the blind fabric, pull the free end of each gathering cord at the top end of the blind and push the fabric away, creating even gathers along each of the three gathering cords. When the ruched blind is the correct length for the window, secure the gathering cords in place at the top of the blind, as in step 4, and trim away the excess cord.

6 Pin the looped part of the hook-and-eye tape ¼" (5mm) from the top edge of the blind on the reverse side, and hand-sew in place.

7 To attach the curtain rings, hand-sew one at the bottom of each channel, then sew on another two at even intervals between the top and bottom of the blind, so that you end up with three rings along the length of each channel. (If your window is very tall, you may need to use more than three rings per channel.)

Knot the lifting cords securely onto the rings at the bottom of each channel, and feed them through the remaining two rings.

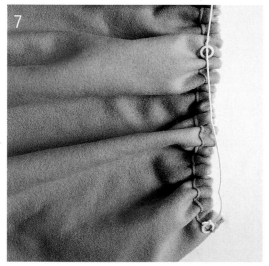

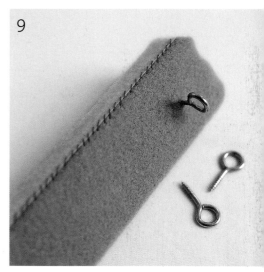

8 Wrap the wooden batten with matching fabric, and staple it in place using a staple gun. Pin, then hand-sew the soft part of the hook-and-eye tape along the edge of the fabric-covered batten.

9 Attach one screw eye ³⁄₄" (2cm) from each end of the top of the batten and another in the middle.

Screw the batten onto the top of the window frame, and attach the cleat at one side of the window. To hang up the blind, feed the lifting strings through the screw eyes from left to right or from right to left, depending on which side of the window you have attached the cleat.

bold **flower pillow**

The gathering technique used here elevates a graphic flower design into a bold three-dimensional statement, representing nature at its most colorful. The magenta felt used for the petals has a density and strength that allows them to stand up without the need for additional support from batting. You can pad the petals with batting if you wish, but it will create a slightly harder, more rigid look and feel.

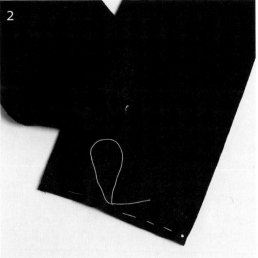

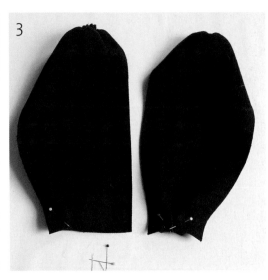

materials + tools
FEATHER PILLOW INSERT, 18 x 18"
    (45 x 45CM)
FOR THE PILLOW COVER: 19 x 39½"
    (47 x 97CM) CREAM FELT OR
    FELTED WOVEN-WOOL FABRIC
FOR THE CONTRASTING FLOWER: 18 x
    20" (45 x 50CM) MAGENTA FELT
    OR FELTED WOVEN-WOOL FABRIC
MATCHING ZIPPER, 18" (45CM) LONG
    (OPTIONAL—SEE PAGES 126–127)
MATCHING SEWING THREAD
BASIC SEWING KIT
SEWING MACHINE

1 If you wish to make a pillow back with a zipper, cut three pieces of cream felt—one for the pillow front measuring 19 x 19" (47 x 47cm) and two for the pillow back measuring 19 x 10½" (47 x 25.5cm) and 19 x 10" (47 x 24.5cm). If you wish to make a sewn-in pillow back, cut the back panel to the same measurements as the front.

Cut five pieces of magenta felt for the petals measuring 17½ x 4" (45 x 10cm).

2 Hand sew a gathering thread along one end of each petal, sewing ⅝" (1.5cm) in from the edge. Gently pull the thread to gather the end of the petal tightly, and knot securely on the reverse.

3 Form a box pleat at the other end of each petal by folding both sides inward so that the folds meet in the center; pin and tack in place.

previous spread The tightly gathered edge of each petal is stitched at the center of the pillow in a circular form, making it look as if the petals are growing out of the fabric base.

4 Draw a circle measuring 2" (5cm) in diameter in the middle of the front panel of the pillow.

5 Pin and tack the gathered end of the five petals around the circle so that they fan outward to create a flower shape. Fold the gathered ends under to create a neat, raised center for the flower; machine-sew in place on the reverse of each petal.

6 Pin and tack the box pleated end of each petal to the edge of the square pillow front.
    Make up the pillow back and join the front and back as described on page 126 or 127.

pillow with **rosette clusters**

Inspired, in part, by my diving vacations on coral reefs in the South China Sea, this design has a vital, dynamic quality, as the three-dimensional effect plays tricks with the eyes. The wonderful texture and depth of color have been created by folding small circles of bright orange cloth (either felt or felted wool) and packing them very tightly together on the base fabric in order to create a structure that seems alive, and screams out to be stroked.

materials + tools
FEATHER PILLOW INSERT, 10 x 18" (25 x 45CM)
FOR THE PILLOW COVER: 23½ x 19" (57 x 47CM)
    ORANGE FELT OR FELTED WOVEN-WOOL FABRIC
FOR THE FOLDED ROSETTES: 20 x 18" (50 x 45CM)
    ORANGE FELT OR FELTED WOVEN-WOOL FABRIC
MATCHING ZIPPER, 18" (45CM) LONG
    (OPTIONAL—SEE PAGES 126–127)
MATCHING SEWING THREAD
BASIC SEWING KIT
SEWING MACHINE

1 If you wish to make a pillow back with a zipper, cut out three pieces of felt for the pillow cover—one piece measuring 11 x 19" (27 x 47cm) for the front and two pieces measuring 6 x 19" (14.5 x 47cm) and 6½ x 19" (15.5 x 47cm) for the back. If you wish to make a sewn-in pillow back, cut the back panel to the same measurements as the front.

To make the rosettes, cut out 60 felt circles with a 3" (7cm) diameter.

2 Pinch each felt circle in the middle, and fold the sides in to form a rosette. Hand-stitch the base of each folded rosette to hold it together.

opposite This stunning decorative pillow creates a colorful textural statement in any room. The design inspiration of the coral is evident, both in the vibrant shades of orange and in the gorgeous tactile surface that you cannot help but touch.

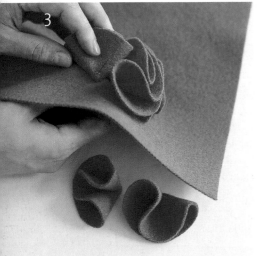

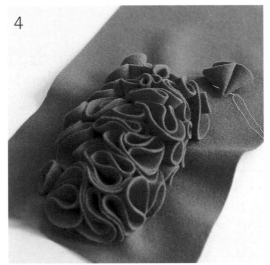

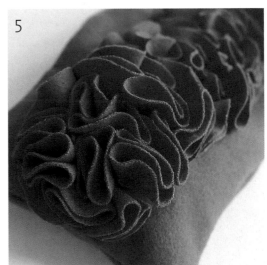

3 Starting at one end of the front pillow panel, hand-stitch the rosettes onto the fabric, stitching neatly and securely through the base of each one.

4 Continue adding rosettes, positioning them very close together to form a dense, wide row of rosettes through the center of the pillow panel. Make sure that the row of rosettes is straight and that there is the same amount of undecorated base fabric on either side of the row.

5 Make up the pillow back and join the front and back as described on page 126 or 127. Insert the pillow form into the finished cover.

pleats + folds

pleats + folds

THERE ARE NUMEROUS PLEATING TECHNIQUES COMMONLY USED IN BOTH CLOTHING AND SOFT FURNISHING DESIGN. IN GARMENTS, PLEATS ARE USED TO ALLOW MOVEMENT; IN SOFT FURNISHINGS AND UPHOLSTERY, THEY ADD FULLNESS. I HAVE USED A VARIETY OF PLEATING TECHNIQUES IN THIS CHAPTER TO ACHIEVE DIFFERENT LOOKS.

> Pleating is a versatile technique that can be used in its various forms to add fullness, texture, and a three-dimensional effect to heavy felt and felted woven-wool fabrics.

There are sharp pressed knife pleats, box pleats, and pinch pleats, as well as a simple tucking technique where the small pleats are stitched through their entire length. I have also included different variations of rolled tubular pleats, which work very well with heavy felt fabrics.

A simple knife pleat has been used for the Pleated Vase Cover (see pages 42–43). These pleats are sewn, then pressed into place using a hot iron, and the pleated strip is then stitched onto the base fabric that covers the entire vase. Using felt with a small synthetic fiber content is preferable for this project, as the pleats will be sharper and more permanent than with 100 percent wool felt or felted woven cloth, which will form softer pleats. A pleated felt trim such as this could be added to other items, too—a decorative pillow front or table runner, for example—as a simple way to add texture.

Staggered rows of small tucks used to gather the top and bottom edges of the Pleated Drum Lampshade (see pages 52–55) create an interesting diagonal fold in the middle of the shade. This is a great way to revamp an old shade or add interest to a plain one. Felt gives a warm ambient light, but remember that pale colors will let more light through than dark tones.

Pleating techniques such as box pleats, pinch pleats, and goblet pleats are traditionally used to gather curtain headings. These techniques can also be used to add fullness and texture to other soft-furnishing items—for example, I used a row of repeated box pleats on a felt Box Pleat Throw (see pages 60–61). As both sides of the box pleat look great, this technique works very well when used as a simple decoration on a reversible throw.

Tubular rolled pleats work very well in felt. The pleats are created by folding the fabric and sewing it in place with a running stitch along the entire length of the cloth to form a tube. For the Pleated Magazine Holder (see pages 56–59), I have used the rolled-pleat technique in its most simplistic form. The tubular pleats are sewn into the front strip at random intervals. To form the handy pockets in which to store away and organize magazines, loose papers, and envelopes, a separate back panel is then sewn onto the front strip at the top and bottom, and attached in places by sewing over some of the pleat seams on the front strip. The pockets can be made smaller or larger by moving these seams closer or farther away from each other. This simple design also makes an attractive wall hanging in its own right.

Tubular pleats are used on a much larger scale for the Snipped-Pleat Throw (see pages 62–65), which requires quite a lot of sewing. The pleats are sewn at intervals across the width of the throw, with a large flat area in the middle. After all the pleats have been sewn in place, each pleat is snipped into small notches using sharp scissors, creating a row of small loops that form a fun organic design. This throw, like a number of other projects, could be given a softer appearance by machine-washing it at a hot temperature. If you wish to do this, bear in mind that different felts react differently, and different water temperatures will give varied results, so try a small sample swatch first to make sure that the end result is what you intend.

Tubular pleats can be stuffed with strips of foam or batting to make them rounder. For the Pillow with Padded Pleat Detail (see pages 48–51), the stuffed pleats have been pinched together and stitched at intervals. On the Multicolored Wall Panel (see pages 44–47), the seam allowances have been pushed inside each pleat on the reverse side, to help the pleats stand off the base fabric.

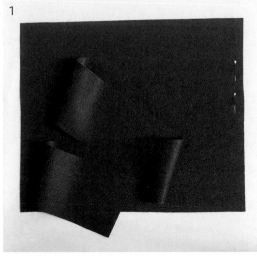

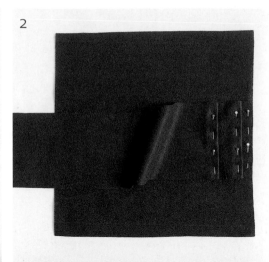

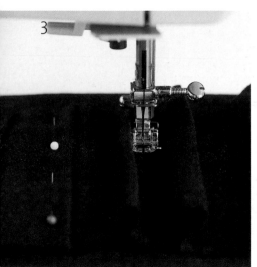

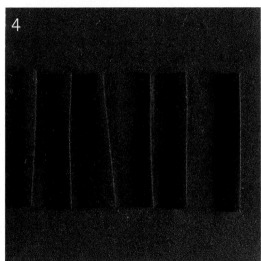

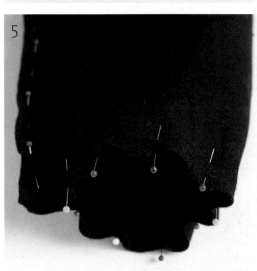

materials + tools

FOR THE VASE COVER: A RECTANGLE OF
PURPLE FELT (WOOL/POLYESTER MIX)
THE HEIGHT AND CIRCUMFERENCE
OF THE VASE PLUS ½" (1CM) SEAM
ALLOWANCE; A CIRCLE THE
DIAMETER OF THE VASE PLUS ½"
(1CM) SEAM ALLOWANCE

FOR THE PLEATED TRIM: A STRIP OF
PURPLE FELT (WOOL/POLYESTER
MIX) 4" (10CM) WIDE AND TWICE
THE CIRCUMFERENCE OF THE VASE

MATCHING SEWING THREAD

BASIC SEWING KIT & SEWING MACHINE

1 Lay the rectangle of felt for the vase cover on the work surface. Pin one end of the felt strip one-third of the way down one short side, lining up the edges of the two pieces of felt.

2 Fold the felt strip over to form overlapping pleats, pinning them in place as you go—the gaps between pleats can be random. Work all the way to the end of the strip of felt, making sure that the edge of the strip and the edge of the vase cover align when you reach the end.

3 Machine-sew each pleat to the base fabric underneath the overlap, so that the stitching is concealed by the pleat. You will need to remove the pins before you sew each pleat in place.

4 Press the pleats down with a hot iron, to create sharp edges.

5 Fold the cover in half lengthwise with right sides facing, and pin then machine-sew the sides together along the ½" (1cm) seam allowance. Again, using the ½" (1cm) seam allowance, pin and then machine-sew the circular base to the bottom of the cover. Cut V-shaped notches in the seam allowance around the base to allow the fabric to spread. Turn the cover right side out, then insert the vase.

pleated vase cover

This simple felt cover will transform the look of a
cylindrical vase or make a unique wine bottle cover.
Not only does it create an interesting shape with
matte texture, but the felt will also act as a protective
cover. This technique offers different design options—
you may want the pleat detail to extend the full length
of the vase, for example, although I feel it works
best when it covers no more than one-third of the vase.

multicolored wall panel

A wall panel can be a great way to add a splash of color to plain walls. Use whatever color combination you desire in order to draw out and emphasize the themes and tones that are already present in your interior. When stretching the fabric over the wooden backing board of your panel, make sure that it is straight and as tight as possible, with a uniform tension: this will ensure an even, crisp finish.

materials + tools

22 x 17½" (55 x 44CM) RED FELT OR FELTED
    WOVEN-WOOL FABRIC
22 x 13½" (55 x 34CM) MAGENTA FELT OR
    FELTED WOVEN-WOOL FABRIC
22 x 14¼" (55 x 36CM) BLUE FELT OR FELTED
    WOVEN-WOOL FABRIC
22 x 12" (55 x 30CM) BLACK FELT OR FELTED
    WOVEN-WOOL FABRIC
18 x 39" (45 x 100CM) OF ¾"- (2CM-) THICK
    POLYESTER BATTING
WOODEN BOARD, 18 x 39" (45 x 100CM)
BLACK SEWING THREAD
BASIC SEWING KIT
SEWING MACHINE
STAPLE GUN AND STAPLES

1 Work out your design and cut out the strips of felt accordingly. We used two strips of red felt measuring 8¾ x 22" (22 x 55cm); two strips of magenta felt, one measuring 4¾ x 22" (12 x 55cm) and one measuring 8½ x 22" (22 x 55cm); three strips of blue felt measuring 4¾ x 22" (12 x 55cm); and six strips of black felt measuring 2 x 22" (5 x 55cm).

2 Lay the strips of felt alongside each other in your chosen order, with the wrong side facing up and separating each bright color with a narrow black strip. Pin and then, using black thread, machine-sew the strips together along a ½" (1cm) seam allowance.

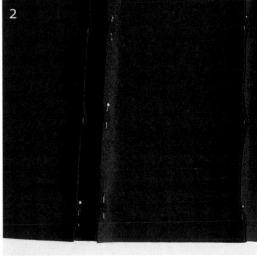

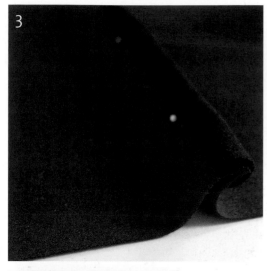

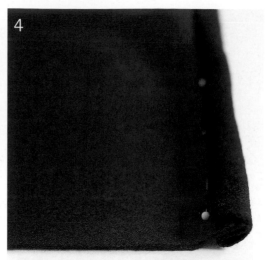

opposite The seam allowance has been tucked inside the "tubes" that divide the block colors— this allows them to stand proud and create the raised detail.

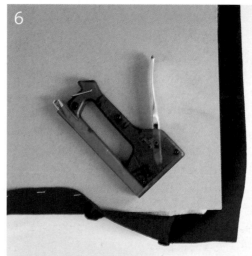

3 Turn the joined fabric strips over, so that the new multicolored fabric is right side up. Pinch the seams of each black strip together, forming a fold; pin the fold in place all the way along each black strip. The seams that join the strips of felt together will be concealed within the fold of black felt, as with a French seam—this helps to accentuate the raised three-dimensional effect.

4 Machine-sew carefully along the edge of each black strip, joining the adjacent colored strips together and securing the folds in place. Sew as close to the edge of the black strip as possible so that the stitching is less visible.

5 Lay the piece of batting on top of the wooden board, making sure that the edges align neatly. Lay the piece of multicolored felt right side up on top of the batting, and ensure that it is completely straight.

6 Being careful not to let the batting and fabric slip, turn the board over. Starting in the center of one long side, fold the edge of the felt over the board, and staple it in place on the back. Stretch the fabric taut from the opposite side, and staple in place. Continue around the board, working outward from the center and alternating sides, to ensure an even tension all over.

pillow with **padded pleat detail**

The stuffed pleats that decorate one side of this smart pillow have been pinched at various intervals to create a clean-cut design. You may decide not to pinch the pleats, but instead leave them as continuous tubes. I have covered only half of the pillow front with detailing, creating a balance between the flat area and the raised panel. For a more textured look, you can add more pleats or even cover the entire front surface of the pillow with them. This design would also work well on a rectangular pillow.

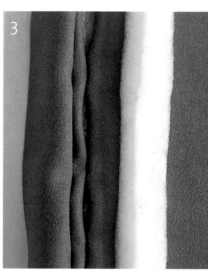

materials + tools

FEATHER PILLOW INSERT, 18 x 18"
   (45 x 45CM)

48½ x 19" (122 x 47CM) BLUE FELT OR
   FELTED WOVEN-WOOL FABRIC

4 x 20" (10 x 50CM) OF ¾"- (2CM-)
   THICK FOAM OR POLYESTER BATTING

MATCHING ZIPPER, 18" (45CM) LONG
   (OPTIONAL—SEE PAGES 126–127)

MATCHING SEWING THREAD

BASIC SEWING KIT

SEWING MACHINE

1 If you wish to make a pillow back with a zipper, cut three pieces of felt for the pillow cover—one for the front measuring 28 x 19" (72 x 47cm) and two for the back measuring 19 x 10½" (47 x 25.5cm) and 19 x 10" (47 x 24.5cm). If you wish to make a sewn-in pillow back, cut the back panel 19 x 19" (47 x 47cm) .

Cut five strips of foam or batting measuring 19 x ¾" (47 x 2cm).

2 Lay the front panel of the cushion cover horizontally on your work surface, with the right side facing up. Using tailor's chalk and a metal ruler, mark out the first 2" (5cm) pleat 3" (8cm) in from one side. Mark four more 2" (5cm) pleats, leaving a gap of 1¼" (3cm) between them.

3 Turn the felt over, and place a strip of foam or batting inside a pleat, folding the felt around it.

opposite The raised detail on the front of this pillow cover creates interesting effects of light and shadow between the folds of the padded pleats.

4 Turn the fabric over with the strip of foam or batting still in position in the center of the pleat marks. Pin the felt together around the foam or batting, encasing it inside the pleat. Make sure that the ends of the strip align with the edges of the felt, and follow the marked lines as a guide as you pin down their length. Fill and pin the remaining pleats in the same way.

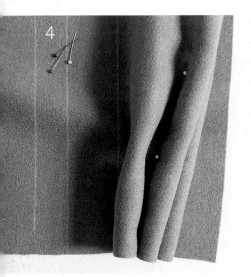 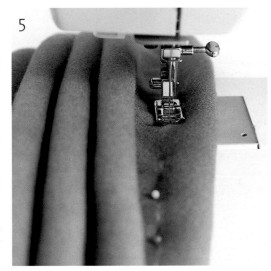 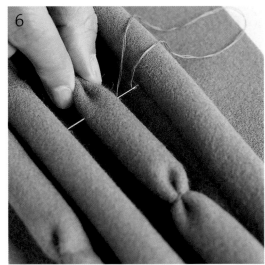

5 Using a straight stitch and matching thread, machine-sew along the marked lines to close the five padded pleats, removing the pins as you sew.

6 Pinch the top of each pleat together at random intervals along its length to form a neat tuck, and hand-stitch these in place using a needle and matching thread.

Make up the pillow back and join the front and back as described on page 126 or 127. Insert the pillow form into the finished cover.

pleated drum lampshade

The pleats around the top and bottom edges of this lampshade are
positioned at staggered intervals to form the felt "pillow" between
them in the middle section of the shade, which creates an interesting
undulating shape. The felt cover is simply slipped over a standard
white or cream drum lampshade, available from department stores.
If you are using a different-sized shade, remember to adjust the
measurements, including the length of the pleats, to suit the proportions.

materials + tools

BASIC WHITE OR CREAM PAPER DRUM LAMPSHADE,
   9" (23CM) DIAMETER, 7" (18CM) HIGH
37¼ x 7" (95 x 18CM) ORANGE FELT
   OR FELTED WOVEN-WOOL FABRIC
MATCHING SEWING THREAD
BASIC SEWING KIT
SEWING MACHINE

1 Lay the felt rectangle on your work surface.
Starting at the left short edge of the felt,
measure 1¾" (4cm) along the top edge, and
mark the first ¾"- (2cm-) wide pleat with tailor's
chalk. Measure 2¾" (7cm) in from this, and mark
the next ¾"- (2cm-) wide pleat. Continue until
you reach the other side of the felt—you will end
up with ten pleats. Mark pleats along the bottom
edge of the felt in the same way, but this time
marking the first ¾"- (2cm-) wide pleat 3" (8cm)
from the left edge. Measure 2¾" (7cm) in from
this and mark the next pleat. Continue marking
pleats at 2¾" (7cm) intervals until you reach the
other side. Measure 3" (8cm) toward the center
of the fabric from the middle of each pleat, and
mark the end of the pleat with a pin.

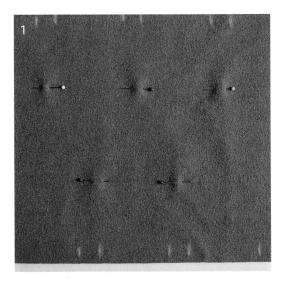

opposite Both funky and uplifting, this orange lampshade makes a bold statement in an understated minimalist interior and casts a warm, welcoming light.

2 Working along the top and bottom edges of the felt in turn, pinch each pleat together, and hold in place with a pin.

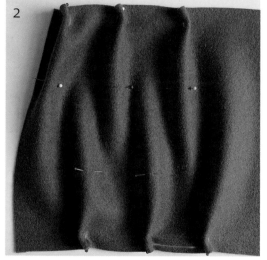

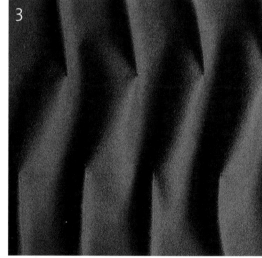

3 Using a straight stitch and matching thread, machine-sew each pleat in place, tapering down to where the end point is marked with a pin. Make sure your stitching is neat and even, as it will be on the outside of the finished shade.

4 Using a ½" (1cm) seam allowance, pin the two short sides of the felt rectangle together with the pleats facing inward. Check that the cover will fit snugly over the lampshade and adjust the seam allowance if necessary, then machine-sew. Turn the cover right side out and slip it over the shade. Hand-stitch the inside of the pleats to the rim of the shade in a few places to secure.

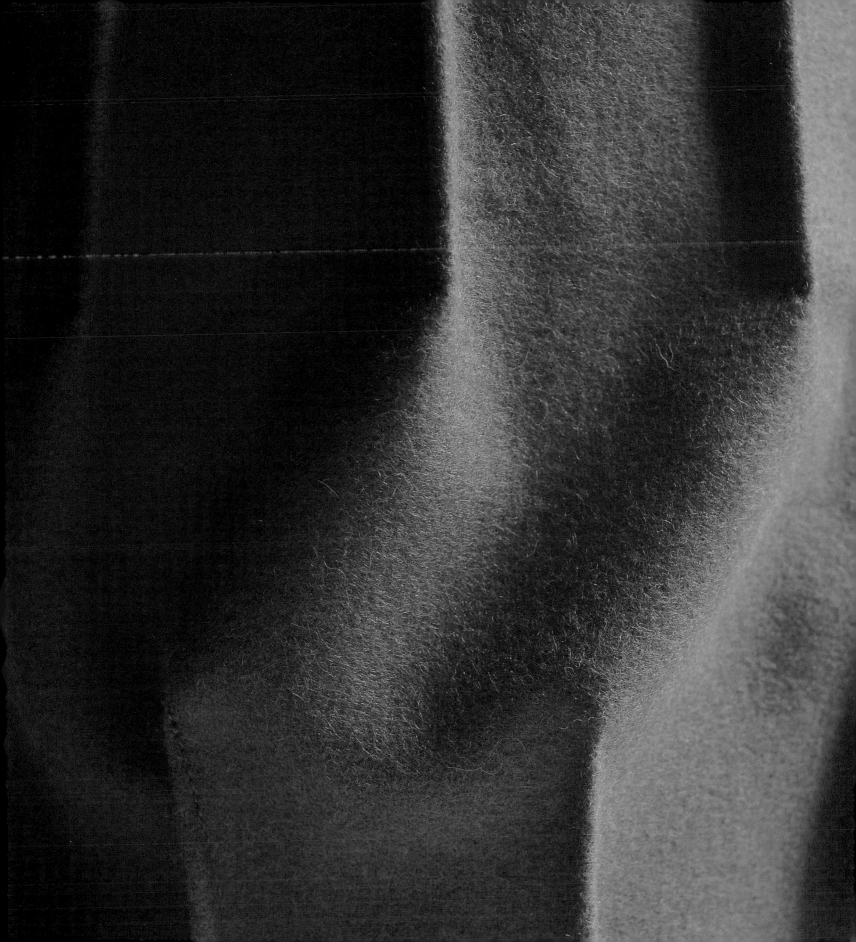

pleated magazine holder

A functional project as well as a decorative one, this attractive pleated wall hanging, in sophisticated dark elephant-gray felt, is ideal for organizing magazines, books, catalogs, letters, or other paperwork. The pleats should be spaced randomly, as this will create interest and give the piece individuality. The pleats are attached to the backing fabric at different points to form pockets for storage, so you can vary the size of the pockets to suit your storage needs.

materials + tools
40 x 40" (1 x 1M) DARK GRAY FELT
   OR FELTED WOVEN-WOOL FABRIC
MATCHING SEWING THREAD
BASIC SEWING KIT
SEWING MACHINE

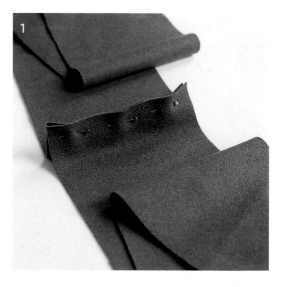

1 Cut 8"- (20cm-) wide strips of felt to make two long pieces for the front and back of the magazine holder—the strip for the flat back piece should measure 72" (180cm) in length and the strip for the pleated front piece should measure 108" (270cm) in length. You will need to join two or three pieces together to create the continuous long lengths; do this by pinning the strips end to end, and machine-sewing a ½" (1cm) seam.

previous page This pleated magazine holder makes a great decorative wall hanging for any room and looks good even when the pockets are empty.

2 Using a metal ruler and tailor's chalk, mark guidelines for the horizontal pleats all the way along the long front piece. Start at one end, and mark the first pleat 2½" (6cm) in from the edge of the fabric. Allow a width of 1¼" (3cm) for each pleat, and mark a total of six pleats, leaving gaps of 1¼" (3cm), 2" (5cm), 6" (15cm), 1¼" (3cm), and ¾" (2cm) between the pleats.

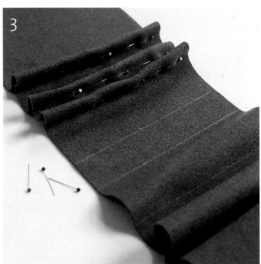

Leave a gap of 8" (20cm), then repeat the set of pleats again, either keeping the same size gaps between the pleats as before, or changing the spacing to create a more random design. Continue marking sets of pleats until you reach the end of the fabric.

3 When all the guidelines have been marked, pinch the 1¼"- (3cm-) wide pleats together, and pin them in place along their length.

When all the pleats have been pinned, check that the front and back pieces are the same length—either trim off the excess fabric or adjust the pleats as necessary.

4 Using a short straight stitch and matching sewing thread, machine-sew all of the pleats in place, removing the pins as you work. Knot all of the loose threads securely, then carefully trim off the ends for a neat finish.

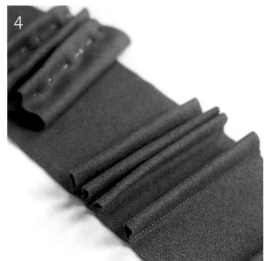

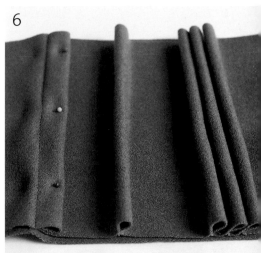

5 Place the front and back pieces of felt with right sides together—with the pleats facing inward—and pin them along the top and bottom edges; machine-sew a ½" (1cm) seam along both ends. Secure the threads and trim, then turn the magazine holder right side out.

6 Lay the magazine holder pleat side up and, using the pleat stitch lines as a guide, machine-sew the front and back strips of felt together at intervals of approximately 12" (30cm), to create the storage pockets. You can vary the size of the pockets depending on what you want them to hold, but always follow the existing stitch lines.

Using a pleat that is usually associated
with curtain headings and valances gives
an elegant look to a simple throw.

box pleat throw

Depending on how you wish to use it, this throw can be made to any size and you can sew more or fewer box pleats, adjusting the measurements to suit your requirements. I used a piece of fabric measuring 44 x 60" (110 x 150cm) for a design featuring three sets of four pleats—the central pleats are 8" (20cm) long and the inner and outer pleats are 10" (25cm) long, with 8" (20cm) between each set. If you wish to add more pleats, add an extra 6" (15cm) to the width measurement for each row of pleats and the gap between rows.

materials + tools
44 x 60" (110 x 150CM) CREAM FELT OR FELTED
    WOVEN-WOOL FABRIC
CONTRASTING TACKING THREAD
MATCHING SEWING THREAD
BASIC SEWING KIT
SEWING MACHINE

1 Lay the fabric on a flat surface with the long side running horizontally, and mark out three sets of four pleats using a ruler and tailor's chalk or a fabric-marker pen. Start with a set of outer pleats, which are 10" (25cm) long and 2" (5cm) wide (when sewn), with a 2" (5cm) gap between each pleat. Draw the first line 11" (27.5cm) down from the top edge of the fabric, and work downward. Mark four 10"- (25cm-) long, 4"- (10cm-) wide pleats, leaving a 2" (5cm) gap between each one, then draw a guideline through the center of each of the four pleats. Leave a 8" (20cm) space from the base of these pleats, and mark out the central set of pleats, which are 8" (20cm) long and 2" (5cm) wide (when sewn), with a 2" (5cm) gap between each pleat as before. Leaving another 8" (20cm) space, mark out the second outer set of 10"- (25cm-) long, 4"- (10cm-) wide pleats.

2 To create the box pleats and the resulting three-dimensional effect between the sets of pleats, pull in the outer edges of each box pleat and align them on the guideline running through the center of the pleat; pin in place.

3 To keep the pleats neat and make sewing easier, tack the folds in place using a needle and tacking thread. Repeat this process for all the pleats so that, when the entire row of pleats is tacked, you are left with two 8" (20cm) gaps between each set of pleats.

4 Machine-sew the pleats, stitching ¼" (5mm) in from the folded edge all the way down one edge, across the bottom of the pleat and then up the other side. Carefully remove all tacking.

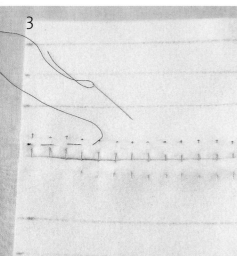

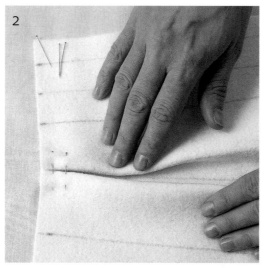

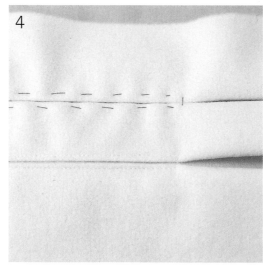

snipped-pleat throw

This gorgeous red throw has been made using the same technique to form the pinch pleats as for the wall-hung magazine holder (see pages 56–59), but a very different look has been created by snipping the pleats at close intervals all the way along. This has resulted in a more fun, soft, and relaxed look that is perfect for a bedroom. Pressed felt does not fray, so the cut edges retain their crisp finish; however, if you machine-wash the throw on a hot cycle, the fabric will shrink slightly and the edges of the snipped pleats will soften.

materials + tools
80 x 58" (200 x 145M) RED FELT
    (OR THE SIZE REQUIRED FOR YOUR BED)
MATCHING SEWING THREAD
BASIC SEWING KIT
SEWING MACHINE

1 Cut a piece of felt to the size you require for your bed—this one is 80" (200cm) wide and 43" (109cm) long when finished. If necessary, you can join two pieces of fabric together, machine-stitching a horizontal seam which can then be incorporated into a pleat. Spread the fabric out on a large flat work surface, and use a metal ruler and tailor's chalk to mark out the guidelines for the horizontal pinch pleats. In this instance, the pleats run parallel to the 80" (200cm) edge of the fabric, and the first is 2½" (6cm) from the edge. Allow 1¼" (3cm) for each pleat and, working toward the center of the throw, mark eight pleats in total, leaving gaps of 1¼" (3cm), 2" (5cm), 1½" (4cm), 1¼" (3cm), ¾" (2cm), 2" (5cm), and ¾" (2cm) between them.

Mark another set of four pleats starting from the opposite long edge of the throw. This time, mark the first pleat 2" (5cm) in from the edge and, working toward the center of the throw as before, leave gaps of 6" (15cm), ¾" (2cm), and ¾" (2cm) between each of the pleats.

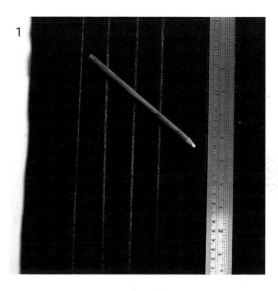

1

opposite Snipping the classic pinch pleats softens the look of the fabric and gives it an organic quality, making the throw more sensuous and inviting.

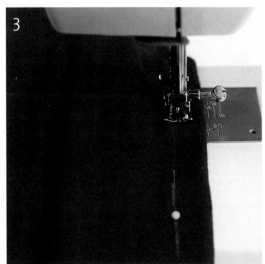

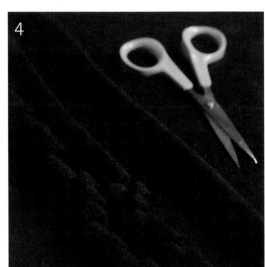

2 When both sets have been marked, pinch the 1¼"- (3cm-) wide pleats together, and pin in place.

3 Using a straight stitch and matching sewing thread, machine-sew along the length of all of the pleats, taking extra care to keep your lines of stitching straight. Knot all of the loose threads securely, then trim off the ends for a neat finish.

4 Using very sharp scissors with pointed tips, snip through the pleats at ½" (1cm) intervals, being careful not to cut through the stitching.
　　To soften the texture of the felt, machine-wash and spin-dry the throw on a hot cycle.

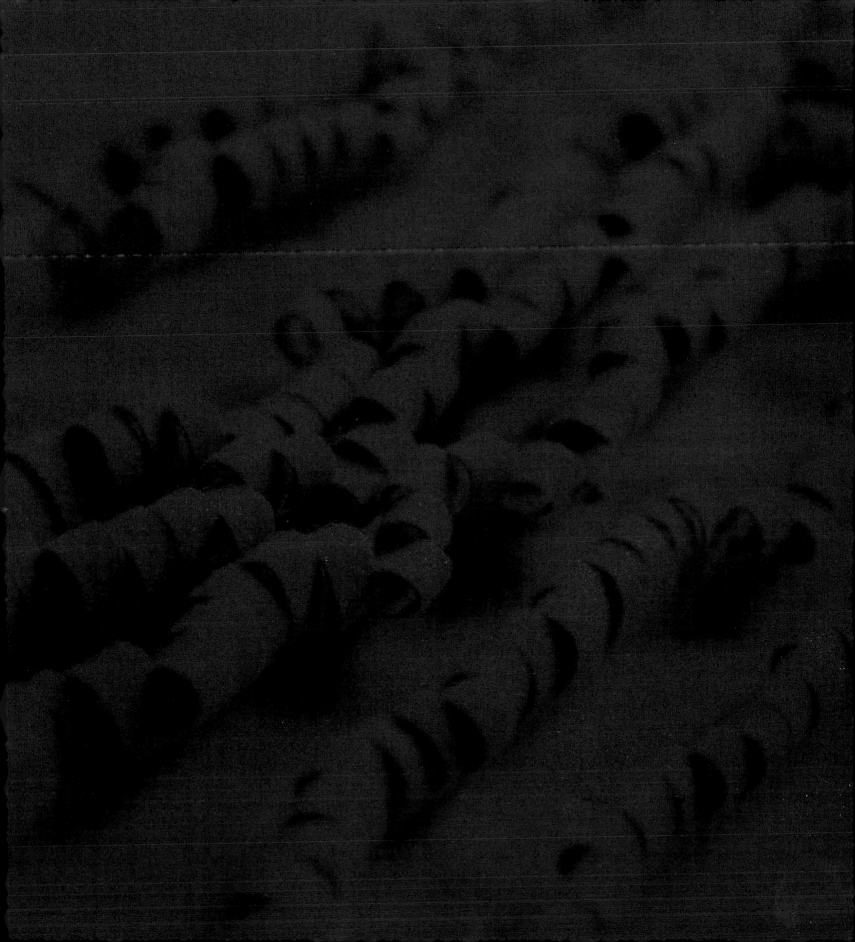

appliqués + cutouts

appliqués + cutouts

APPLIQUÉ IS A SOPHISTICATED WAY OF DESCRIBING THE STITCHING OF DIFFERENT FABRIC ONTO A BACKGROUND TO CREATE A DECORATIVE PATTERN. IN ITS BASIC FORM, IT IS A SIMPLE AND QUICK WAY TO PRODUCE AN INSTANT EFFECT, BUT IT CAN BECOME VERY INVOLVED AND ELABORATE IF YOU LIKE.

Felt has long been appliquéd—the earliest felt appliqué textiles date back to 400BC, though it could be argued that this may have more to do with the way that felt was manufactured than patch and make-do requirements. As a non-woven material, pressed felt is well suited for appliqué—as it does not fray, there is no need to finish the edges or turn them in. To a lesser extent, tightly-woven heavy woolen fabrics fray very little, too, which also makes them suitable for both appliqué and cutout techniques. In addition, both fabrics do not stretch and are easy to work with and, importantly for this chapter, they provide an ideal firm and steady background fabric for appliqué work.

For the following projects I have used basic machine appliqué techniques, where the edges are left raw and the fabric is sewn in place with a straight stitch. The appliqué and cutout motifs are bold and simple, so they can be easily maneuvered on a home sewing machine. Standard cotton or polyester threads can be used, although threads intended for upholstery or soft furnishings are better suited for the heavy, thick fabrics used. This is an important consideration, as the strength of the thread, and therefore the stitch, will hold the felt shapes in place and create a harder-wearing piece. As always, careful preparation is essential. Where applicable, use the templates provided to cut out the shapes to be appliquéd. Move the motifs around on the background fabric until you have found your preferred positioning, then pin or tack them in place to prevent them from moving around when they are being sewn on.

For the multicolored spots on the Doodle Circle Pillow with Stitch Detail (see pages 80–83), batting is used underneath the colored felt circles to raise and accentuate the pattern, which adds a soft sculptural aspect to the pillow. You may wish to experiment with the amount of batting you use in order to get the desired effect. A freehand embroidery technique is used to sew the appliqué shapes firmly in place by overlapping rows of straight stitch around the edge of the circles. As well as securing the motifs to the backing cloth, this technique also creates a fun scribble pattern around the colored spots. A wide zigzag stitch is another alternative, which could be used to create a subtly different effect.

Appliqué motifs can be different shapes and sizes—the techniques are the same—but I prefer a simple elegance that is best achieved by not making the work too fussy.

To make a matching set of table textiles without wasting any fabric, the cutout shapes on the Table Runner (see pages 74–79) are recycled and used as appliqué shapes for the Place Mats (see pages 78–79). After marking the shapes on the top layer of fabric on the table runner, two layers of fabric are stitched together carefully, and the fabric inside each stitched shape is cut out close to the stitch line to reveal the contrasting fabric layer underneath. The cutout shapes are then appliquéd onto the place mats.

The Snowdrift Window Shade (see pages 92–93) is created using a similar cutout technique, which provides a great way to breathe new life into a ready-made shade. A layer of felted woven-wool cloth is sewn on the top of the shade fabric using wavy horizontal lines of straight stitch. The layer of woolen cloth is then cut out close to the stitch lines to reveal the window shade fabric underneath.

A combination of cutout and folding techniques has been used for the Pinched-Petal Lampshade (see pages 84–87) and Curtain with Cut Leaf Border (see pages 88–91). The round shapes are sewn onto the lampshade cover with a simple row of straight stitch, then folded to create a sculptural shape that produces interesting shadows. For the decorative border on the curtain, instead of completely cutting out the leaf shapes, the top layer of fabric is cut halfway, then folded back on itself and attached at the side, revealing the layer of contrasting fabric underneath.

bull's-eye target sofa throw

For this graphic throw I have abstracted the classic bull's-eye target design. Instead of having regular circles of exact proportions in red, white, and blue, the project introduces irregular freehand circles in various shades of gray—from pale cloud, through elephant gray, to deep charcoal—which have been placed on top of one another in a random, off-center way. You can sew more or fewer sets of circles onto the base fabric, if you wish, placing them closer together and even overlapping them, or just sew one set in the center.

materials + tools

FOR THE BASE OF THE THROW: 56 x 56" (140 x 140CM) PALE GRAY FELT OR FELTED WOVEN-WOOL FABRIC
FOR THE APPLIQUÉ CIRCLES: 39 x 56" (100 x 140CM) CHARCOAL FELT OR FELTED WOVEN-WOOL FABRIC; 20 x 20" (50 x 50CM) DARK GRAY FELT OR FELTED WOVEN-WOOL FABRIC; 12 x 56" (30 x 140CM) MEDIUM-GRAY FELT OR FELTED WOVEN-WOOL FABRIC; AND 8 x 56" (20 x 140CM) OF PALE GRAY FELT OR FELTED WOVEN-WOOL FABRIC
MATCHING DARK GRAY SEWING THREAD
BASIC SEWING KIT
SEWING MACHINE

1 Cut a square of pale gray felt for the base of the throw measuring 56 x 56" (140 x 140cm), or sew two or more pieces together to achieve the desired size. For each of the five sets of overlapping layered circles, cut out three or four felt circles in different colors and sizes. Make sure that you alternate the different shades of gray within each set of circles, and always use charcoal felt for the largest circles, as this will show up well against the pale gray background felt. Draw the circles freehand with tailor's chalk to create an irregular, organic effect (see page 72).

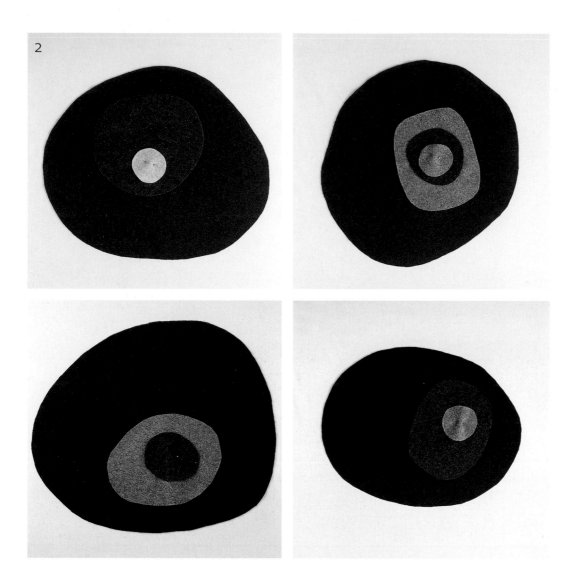

2 Cut the following sets of circles: charcoal circle 20" (50cm) diameter, dark gray circle 8" (20cm) diameter, and light grey circle 3" (7cm) diameter (top left); charcoal circle 16" (40cm) diameter, medium gray circle 10" (25cm) diameter, charcoal circle 6" (15cm) diameter, and medium gray circle 3" (7cm) diameter (top right); charcoal circle 20" (50cm) diameter, medium gray circle 8" (20cm) diameter, and charcoal circle 3" (7cm) diameter (bottom left); charcoal circle 16" (40cm) diameter, dark gray circle 10" (25cm) diameter, and medium gray circle 3" (7cm) diameter (bottom right); charcoal circle 20" (50cm) diameter, dark gray circle 10" (25cm) diameter, and medium gray circle 10" (25cm) diameter (not shown).

Lay all the sets of circles on your work surface, and layer them. Start with the largest charcoal circle at the bottom of each set, and place the medium circle on top, then the smallest circle on top of that. Position each circle off center to create a random design. Play around with the layout of each set until you are happy with the effect, then pin the piles of felt in place.

previous spread The tonal gray color scheme used for this throw is both understated and sophisticated, and will complement neutral modern décor, but you can have lots of fun with this design experimenting with different color combinations.

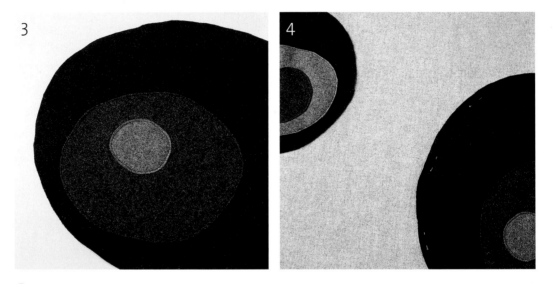

3 Machine-sew each set of circles together, sewing ¼" (5mm) in from the edge of each circle all the way around. Sew the smallest circle into place first, stitching through all three or four layers of felt, then sew the medium-sized circle to the large circle. Make sure that the fabric is flat and smooth as you sew, so that the circles lie flat.

4 Lay the pale gray throw flat on the floor, and place the five stitched circles randomly on top of it; when you are happy with their positions, pin them in place. Machine-sew the sets of circles to the base fabric, sewing ¼" (5mm) in from the edge of the largest circle all the way around.

table runner with
cutout shapes

Wool felt has very good insulating properties and is therefore an
ideal material for table runners and place mats, as it will protect
the tabletop from hot dishes and plates. For this fresh-looking table
runner, I layered two contrasting colors of felt together—cream
and grass green—and used a regular-repeat cutout shape to create
a crisp, orderly design. By using contrasting thread for both the
needle and bobbin, you can make the table runner reversible, with
the stitching creating an attractive pattern.

materials + tools

18 x 80" (45 x 200cm) GREEN FELT OR FELTED
    WOVEN-WOOL FABRIC (OR SHORTER,
    DEPENDING ON THE LENGTH OF YOUR TABLE)
18 x 80" (45 x 200cm) CREAM FELT OR FELTED
    WOVEN-WOOL FABRIC (OR SHORTER, DEPENDING
    ON THE LENGTH OF YOUR TABLE)
CREAM AND GREEN SEWING THREAD
THIN CARDBOARD OR FLEXIBLE PLASTIC SHEET
    TO MAKE THE TEMPLATE
BASIC SEWING KIT
SEWING MACHINE

1 Cut out two pieces of felt in contrasting
colors measuring 18 x 80" (45 x 200cm), or the
required length for your table. (If necessary, you
can create a long strip by joining two or more
shorter pieces together with right sides facing
using a ½" (1cm) seam allowance. In step 2, make
sure you position the leaf shapes an equal
distance on either side of the seam(s).) Lay one
piece of felt on top of the other, aligning the
edges exactly, and pin them together. Machine-
sew all the way around, sewing ¼" (5mm) in
from the edge of the fabric. Thread the sewing
machine with thread in the same color as your
top piece of felt and fill the bobbin with thread
the same color as your bottom piece of felt.

2 Using the template on page 138, draw a trail of leaf shapes along the top surface of the table runner. Check that the following measurements will work for the length of your table runner, taking into account any joining seams, and adjust them as necessary. Start 9½" (24cm) in from one short edge and place the template centrally within the fabric width. Draw a group of six leaves, with 1¼" (3cm) between each one, then leave a 5" (13cm) gap and repeat the set of six, working your way along the whole length, drawing a total of three sets.

opposite Both practical and elegant, a table runner creates a focal point on the table whether it is set or not. The fresh colors would suit a contemporary interior and are perfect for summer, but the design would look equally striking in warmer, moodier colors.

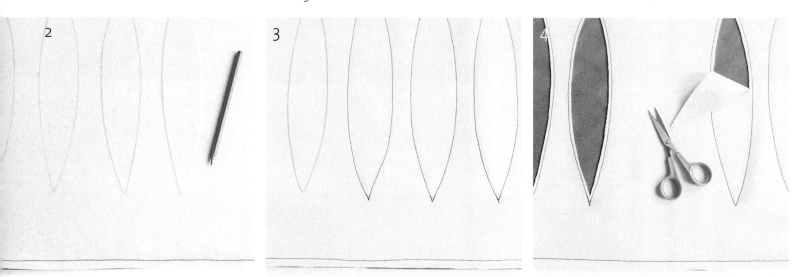

3 Machine-sew along the leaf outlines using straight stitch and contrasting thread.

4 Using sharp, pointed scissors, neatly cut out the top layer of fabric ¼" (5mm) inside the lines of stitching, revealing the contrasting fabric underneath.

place mats with **appliqué shapes**

These place mats have been designed to complement the Table Runner on pages 74–77 and are its direct counterpoint, both in terms of the color combination and in technique. Instead of cutout shapes, I have used appliqué—where the shape is sewn onto the base fabric—to decorate the place mats and have reversed the use of green and cream as the prominent color. If you cut out the cream leaf shapes neatly when making the table runner, you can use them to decorate these place mats.

materials + tools

FOR FOUR PLACE MATS: 28 x 36" (70 x 90CM) GREEN
    FELT OR FELTED WOVEN-WOOL FABRIC
FOR THE APPLIQUÉ SHAPES: 12 x 10" (30 x 25CM)
    CREAM FELT OR FELTED WOVEN-WOOL FABRIC
THIN CARDBOARD OR FLEXIBLE PLASTIC SHEET
    TO MAKE THE TEMPLATE
MATCHING GREEN SEWING THREAD
BASIC SEWING KIT
SEWING MACHINE

1 Use the cream leaf shapes cut out from the Table Runner, or, using the template provided on page 138, draw eight leaf shapes on the piece of cream felt.

2 Neatly cut out the leaf shapes for the appliqué using sharp scissors. Then cut out four pieces of green felt measuring 18 x 14" (45 x 35cm) for the place mats.

3 Pin two leaf shapes onto each place mat. Position each leaf centrally, 1³⁄₄" (4cm) in from each side of the mat.

4 Using green thread for the sewing machine and cream thread for the bobbin, machine-sew with a small straight stitch all the way around the leaf outline, sewing ¹⁄₄" (5mm) in from the edge.

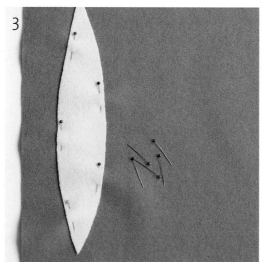

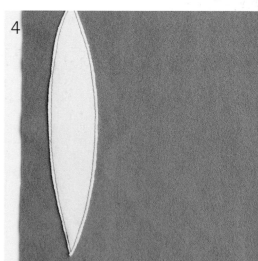

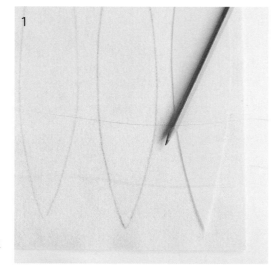

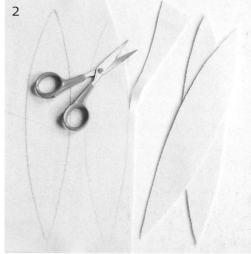

doodle circle pillow
with stitch detail

Although more sophisticated than an average doodle, this technique shows how you can create a unique design for a pillow cover by working simple freehand machine embroidery around brightly-colored felt circles, which are padded with batting to create the raised effect. Try experimenting with other color combinations and different configurations, or you could create different shapes for the padded appliqué.

materials + tools

FEATHER PILLOW INSERT, 18 x 18" (45 x 45CM)

FOR THE PILLOW COVER: 19 x 39½" (47 x 97CM) CREAM FELT OR FELTED WOVEN-WOOL FABRIC

FOR THE APPLIQUÉ CIRCLES: 8 x 8" (20 x 20CM) TURQUOISE FELT OR FELTED WOVEN-WOOL FABRIC; 4 x 4" (10 x 10CM) GREEN FELT OR FELTED WOVEN-WOOL FABRIC; 3 x 3" (8 x 8CM) PINK FELT OR FELTED WOVEN-WOOL FABRIC

12 x 8" (30 x 20CM) OF ¾"- (2CM-) THICK BATTING

MATCHING ZIPPER, 18" (45CM) LONG (OPTIONAL—SEE PAGES 126–127)

RED THREAD FOR THE EMBROIDERY

CREAM THREAD TO MAKE UP THE PILLOW

BASIC SEWING KIT & SEWING MACHINE

1 If you wish to make a pillow back with a zipper, cut three pieces of cream felt for the main body of the pillow cover—one for the front measuring 19 x 19" (47 x 47cm) and two for the back measuring 19 x 10½" (47 x 25.5cm) and 19 x 10" (47 x 24.5cm). If you wish to make a sewn-in pillow back, cut the back panel 19 x 19" (47 x 47cm).

Using tailor's chalk, draw a circle in the center of each piece of colored felt using a small plate, a tumbler, and a smaller glass as guides; cut out.

2 Cut three matching circles of batting, one for each colored felt circle. Trim away ½" (1.5cm) all the way around each circle of batting, so that they are slightly smaller than the felt circles.

opposite The raised circles and stitch detailing create great texture on this playful spotted pillow. The vibrant multicolored circles work best on a white or natural background, but this design would also be successful in a monochromatic color scheme.

3 Work out where you want to position the three colored felt circles on the front panel of the pillow cover. When you are happy with the design, lay the corresponding piece of batting underneath each felt circle, making sure that it is centered, and pin in place.

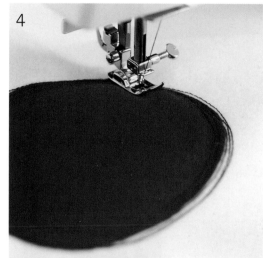
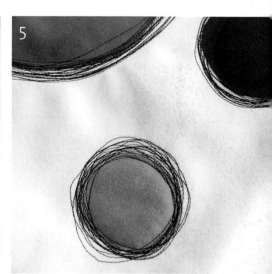

4 Thread the sewing machine with contrasting red thread, and machine-sew the padded circles in place, sewing around and around each circle several times to create a doodle effect. Make sure that each circle is completely secured by stitching.

5 When the appliqué design is complete and all three circles are stitched in place, make up the pillow back and join the front and back as described on page 126 or 127. Insert the pillow form into the finished cover.

pinched-petal lampshade

The cream felt used for this lampshade cover gives out a warm, glowing ambient light. The cutout shapes attached to the surface create interesting depth and shadows. They have been sewn on in a diagonal pattern across the fabric, so that on the finished lampshade they seem like petals or leaves scattered in a breeze. You can easily vary the size, shape, or color of the lampshade to suit your décor.

materials + tools

BASIC WHITE OR CREAM PAPER DRUM LAMPSHADE,
    9" (23CM) DIAMETER, 7" (18CM) HIGH
12 x 30" (30 x 75CM) CREAM FELT OR FELTED
    WOVEN-WOOL FABRIC
THIN CARDBOARD OR FLEXIBLE PLASTIC SHEET
    TO MAKE THE TEMPLATE
MATCHING SEWING THREAD
BASIC SEWING KIT
SEWING MACHINE

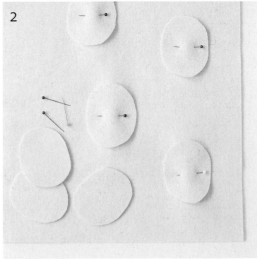

1 Measure the circumference and height of your lampshade, if it is different from the one described above, and cut out a piece of cream felt to your lampshade's measurements, adding an extra ¾–1¼" (2–3cm) to the circumference for the seam allowance. For the lampshade described above, cut a strip of felt measuring 7 x 30" (18 x 75cm).

Using the template on page 139, cut 30 round petal shapes out of the remaining cream felt.

2 Lay the strip of felt on your work surface so that the long sides are running horizontally, and pin the petals onto it. Start near the bottom at one corner, and arrange the petals in diagonal rows that sweep toward the opposite top corner.

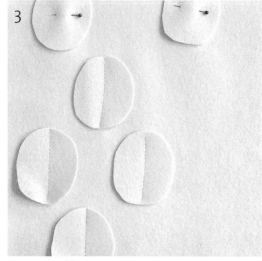

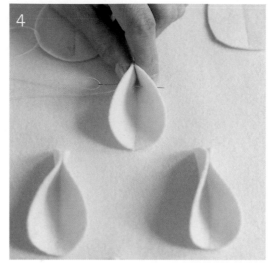

opposite The cutout felt petal shapes, with their edges pinched together to create a three-dimensional effect, make a feature of the lampshade, both when the light is illuminated and when it is not.

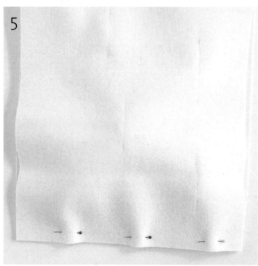

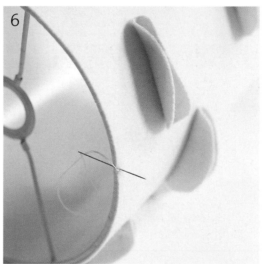

3 Machine-sew each petal down the middle to attach them to the base fabric. Make sure that you sew the petals so that your lines of stitching will run horizontally across the shade, rather than vertically from top to bottom.

4 Pinch the edges of each petal together, and hand-stitch them in the center.

5 With right sides facing, so that the petals are on the inside, fold the strip of felt in half, and pin the short ends together along the ½" (1cm) seam allowance. Check that the cover will fit snugly but easily over the paper lampshade, and adjust

the seam if necessary. Using a straight stitch and matching thread, machine-sew the ends of the base felt together to form a tube.

Trim away any excess fabric from the seam allowance, then press the seam open so that the cover will lie flat against the paper shade.

6 Turn the felt cover right side out, and slip it over the lampshade. Hand-stitch the top and bottom edges of the cover to the shade in a few places to secure it.

curtain with cut leaf border

This double-layered floor-length curtain features a striking leaf design along the bottom, which beautifully accentuates the folds of the richly colored felted wool fabric. The design itself is simplistic, and its effectiveness comes from the repetition of the shapes and the contrasting colors. The leaf shapes have been half cut out and folded back to reveal the cream lining felt underneath. The curtain has been hung using large grommets, but other headings would be equally effective. To determine the size of your curtain, measure from the top of the curtain pole to the floor, and add an extra 2" (5cm) for the heading; measure the width of the window frame and make the curtain one and a half to two times wider than your window to gain the right fullness.

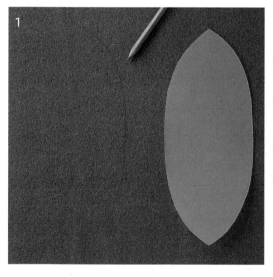

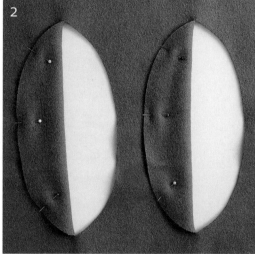

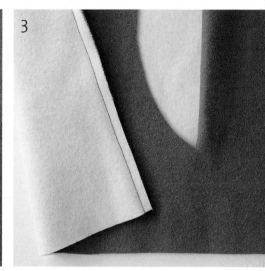

materials + tools

2¼ YDS (2M) OF 60"- (150CM-) WIDE CREAM FELT OR
    FELTED WOVEN-WOOL FABRIC, OR AS REQUIRED
    FOR THE SIZE OF YOUR WINDOW (SEE ABOVE)
2¼ YDS (2M) OF 60"- (150CM-) WIDE ORANGE FELT OR
    FELTED WOVEN-WOOL FABRIC, OR AS REQUIRED
    FOR THE SIZE OF YOUR WINDOW (SEE ABOVE)
6 METAL GROMMETS, 2" (5CM) DIAMETER
THIN CARDBOARD OR FLEXIBLE PLASTIC SHEET TO
    MAKE THE TEMPLATE
MATCHING SEWING THREAD
BASIC SEWING KIT
SEWING MACHINE

1 Using the template on page 140, draw the right-hand half of the leaf shapes along the bottom of the orange fabric, 4" (10cm) up from the edge and with a 2" (5cm) gap between them (adjust this according to the width of your curtain). Leave a ½" (1.5cm) seam allowance on both side edges.

2 Cut out the outlined half of the leaf from top to bottom, and fold the leaf "flap" back on itself; pin in place. Secure by machine-sewing a ½" (1cm) long vertical line in the center of the cut edge.

3 Pin the orange and cream pieces of felt with right sides together, and machine-sew along both sides ½" (1.5cm) in from the edge.

opposite A straightforward cut-and-fold technique has been used to form a decorative border for this curtain, providing interest while remaining clean and unfussy.

4 Turn the curtain right side out. Make sure that both layers of fabric are smooth and flat, then pin them together along the bottom of the curtain to hold them in place temporarily (the bottom of the curtain is left open). Machine-sew the layers together on the right side of each leaf, mirroring the vertical stitch lines described in step 2 and sewing ½" (1cm) in from the right-hand edge of each leaf.

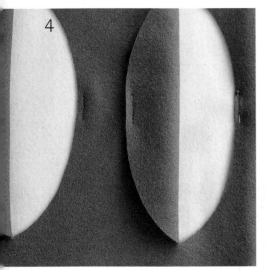 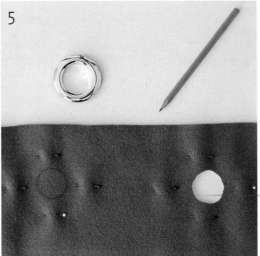 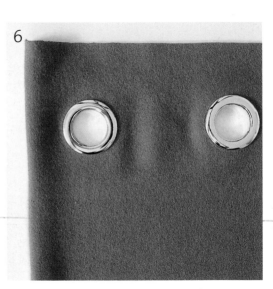

5 To form the grommet heading, ensure that the fabrics are flat and smooth. Mark the positions of the grommets along the top edge of the curtain with tailor's chalk, using the inside of a grommet as a template. Position the grommets 2" (5cm) down from the top edge and 2" (5cm) in from the side edges; leave a gap of about 8" (20cm) between each grommet. Pin the two layers of fabric together around the marked outlines to prevent them from slipping, then cut away the fabric to create holes.

6 Push the grommets into place, snapping the two parts together around the cut edges. Insert the curtain pole through the grommets and hang.

snowdrift window shade

A stylish alternative to curtains, this simple design was inspired by the snowdrifts in my native Finland. A conventional window shade, available from department stores, has been covered with felted wool fabric, which has been stitched and cut out in wave-shaped sections to create the slashed effect. I recommend choosing a pale color for both the shade and felt, as the cutout detail allows light to diffuse softly through the exposed shade and, over time, dyed wool has a tendency to fade when in direct light. The design allows soft light to filter into the room, while retaining privacy.

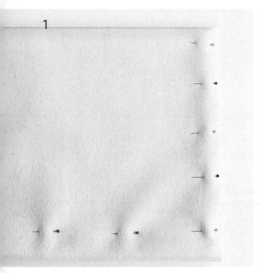

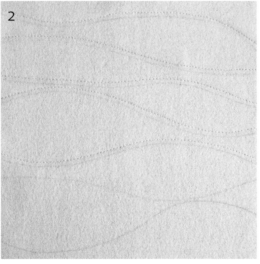

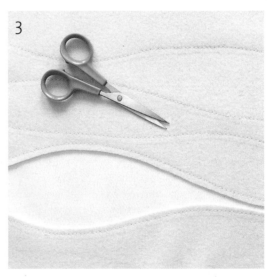

materials + tools

READY-MADE CREAM VINYL
WINDOW SHADE, THE CORRECT
WIDTH FOR YOUR WINDOW
SUFFICIENT CREAM FELT OR FELTED
WOVEN-WOOL FABRIC TO COVER
YOUR SHADE (SEE STEP 1)
MATCHING SEWING THREAD
BASIC SEWING KIT
SEWING MACHINE

1 Cut a piece of felted wool fabric to the size required to cover your window shade when it is fully extended over the window, adding enough to the length to wrap the felt over the bottom edge of the shade, so that it can be stitched in place along the existing seam of the dowel pocket. Pin the felt in place on the window shade fabric, making sure that the edges of the felt are flush with the sides of the shade.

2 Draw random horizontal wavy lines across the felt. (You may wish to draw out your design on paper first, shading in the areas that will be cut out, to check that it works well.) Machine-sew

¼" (5mm) outside of the drawn lines, keeping your lines of stitching an equal distance from the drawn guidelines all the way along.

Machine-sew the overlapped bottom edge of the felt in place, following the existing stitch line of the dowel pocket.

3 Using sharp scissors, neatly cut away the felt between alternate pairs of wavy lines, so that you end up with a wavy band of felt, then a wavy band of exposed shade fabric, and so on. Cut along the drawn guidelines, ¼" (5mm) inside the lines of stitching, and take care not to cut through the shade fabric underneath.

strips + slices

strips + slices

BRIGHTLY COLORED RIBBONS HAVE BEEN USED TO DECORATE CLOTHING AND INTERIOR TEXTILES FOR CENTURIES, EITHER TO ELEVATE THEM FROM THE ORDINARY OR TO ACCENTUATE ASPECTS OF THEIR DESIGN. WHAT WE THINK OF AS "RIBBONS" ARE GENERALLY MADE FROM SILK OR SYNTHETIC FIBERS, BUT THIS IS A RELATIVELY MODERN INTERPRETATION.

> Strips of felt can be sewn or woven together, or used in numerous ways as surface decoration, while slicing techniques can be used to reveal a contrasting layer of fabric underneath.

Originally "ribbon" was simply a thin strip of cloth, which could be applied to furnishings—or indeed garments—in many different practical and decorative ways. This chapter offers a variety of projects based on the theme of slices and strips of felt and heavy felted woolen cloth, which are essentially used as decorative "ribbons" to create pieces with crisp simple lines and an updated modern feel.

The techniques used within this chapter—and throughout this entire book—are very versatile, so you should not feel limited to using them only in the context in which they have been shown. Instead, think of them as a springboard of ideas, and experiment with your own designs. For example, if you like a technique I have used for a throw, but would prefer to make a smaller-scale project such as a decorative pillow, you will find that the same method of fabric manipulation can be adapted and used successfully in a number of different projects.

As previously mentioned, one of the great characteristics of wool felt (which it shares to a very large extent with heavy felted woven-wool cloth) is that it does not fray when cut. As a result, there is no need to finish the edges of the fabric, making felt in many ways the ideal material to be used in the form of strips or slices. For many of the projects in this chapter, you are able to use narrow scraps of felt, or the selvedge strips, which might otherwise have been discarded.

I have included two larger-scale projects in this chapter, in which strips of contrasting felt are used to add color and texture. In the first of these, the Tab-Top Curtain with Layered

below Strips of contrasting felt have been layered between two pieces of the main fabric and sewn together to create reversible, three-dimensional seams, with the stitching visible on only one side.

Strip Detail (see pages 102–105), different colored felt strips are layered together and used to decorate a large piece of plain fabric, while also performing a function by forming the top loops from which the curtain hangs. This layered strip technique is also very effective for decorating large-scale projects such as bedspreads or wall hangings, as the continuous unbroken lines appear as raised stripes on the surface of the cloth.

The second large-scale project is the Throw with Contrasting Strips (see pages 118–121), which could be used as a runner along the end of the bed or scaled up to make a full size bedspread. For this project, the main cloth is cut into wide slices, and the strips of contrasting felt are sandwiched between two layers of the main cloth, creating a reversible seam that gives additional flexibility when the throw is being used. The bold raised effect is present on both sides of the finished throw, but the effect created on the reverse side presents a layered, seamless look. This technique works well for other large projects, such as curtains and room dividers, or indeed wall hangings (although, of course, with a wall hanging, you will not be able to appreciate the reversible nature of the design).

For the Ottoman with Spiral Detail (see pages 114–117), I have taken a different approach, using sliced felt to create texture and reveal the contrasting fabric underneath. The batting used under the base fabric pushes the strips up, enhancing the three-dimensional effect and adding softness. This technique would also work well for a round pillow cover or upholstered seating. It is worthwhile remembering that the use of batting, foam, and other padding can give a dramatically different look and feel to many of the projects.

Long strips of felt scraps can, with very little sewing, be used to create a stylish and artistic Wavy Strips Wall Hanging (see pages 112–113). This simple but extremely effective technique requires almost no technical skill beyond a good eye for color and proportion, especially in relation to the dimensions of the space for which the hanging is intended.

woven felt pillow cover

This pillow cover is made by weaving padded strips of felt together to form a random crisscross pattern—a great technique for using up scraps. The padding gives fullness to the plain weave and the strips are made by sandwiching batting between two layers of colored felt and stitching along both sides, leaving the seam allowance visible on the outside (which can be further accented by using contrasting thread). If you are making more than one woven pillow, give each a unique color balance by changing the number of strips used in each color.

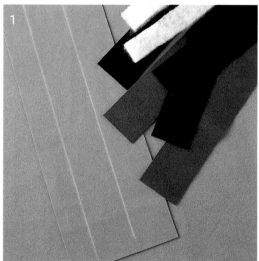

materials + tools

FEATHER PILLOW INSERT, 20 x 20"
   (50 x 50CM)
FOR THE PILLOW COVER: 21 x 43½"
   (52 x 107CM) LIGHT OLIVE FELT OR
   FELTED WOVEN-WOOL FABRIC
FOR THE STRIPS: 30 x 22" (72 x 55CM)
   LIGHT OLIVE AND DARK OLIVE FELT
   OR FELTED WOVEN-WOOL FABRIC;
   25 x 22" (60 x 55CM) NAVY FELT
   OR FELTED WOVEN-WOOL FABRIC
20 x 30" (50 x 80CM) OF ¾"- (2CM-)
   THICK BATTING
MATCHING ZIPPER, 20" (50CM) LONG
   (OPTIONAL—SEE PAGES 126–127)
MATCHING OR CONTRASTING THREAD
BASIC SEWING KIT
SEWING MACHINE

1 If you wish to make a pillow back with a zipper, cut one piece of light olive felt for the pillow front measuring 21 x 21" (52 x 52cm) and two pieces for the pillow back measuring 21 x 11½" (52 x 28cm) and 21 x 11" (52 x 27cm). If you wish to make a sewn-in pillow back, cut the back panel to the same measurements as the front.

Using a ruler and tailor's chalk, mark and cut out a total of 34 strips of felt in three contrasting colors, measuring 2½ x 22" (6 x 55cm) each. For the pillow shown, I cut 12 strips each of light and dark olive, and 10 strips of navy. Cut 17 strips of batting measuring 1¾ x 20" (4.5 x 50cm).

2 Lay a felt strip on your work surface, and center a strip of batting on top of it. Cover the batting with another matching piece of felt, lining up the edges of the strips, and pin the layers together, leaving an equal seam allowance along both sides and at the ends. Using either matching or contrasting thread, machine-sew the two layers of felt together, stitching along both sides, ¼" (5mm) in from the edge, enclosing the batting inside the felt. Repeat this process to make a total of 17 padded felt strips.

opposite The mix of three coordinating colors and the simple basketweave design gives the front of this pillow cover a pixelated look.

3 Lay the 21 x 21" (52 x 52cm) piece of felt for the pillow front on the work surface, and place nine padded strips vertically on top of it. Lay the strips close together, overlapping each other very slightly, and alternate the colors randomly. Pin, then tack, the strips to the top and bottom edges of the base fabric.

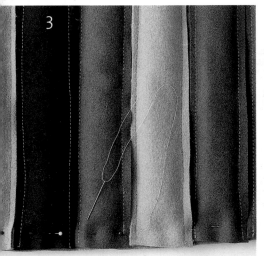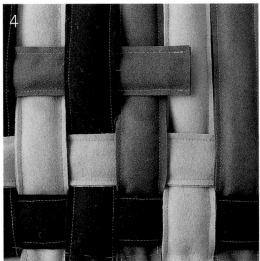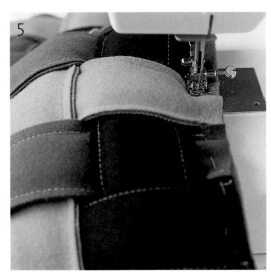

4 Weave the remaining eight strips across the pillow front. Working from left to right, take the first horizontal strip under, then over the fixed vertical strips; take the second horizontal strip over, then under the vertical strips, and so on, alternating the colors randomly as before.

When all the horizontal strips are woven, make sure that they are flat and neat, then pin and tack the ends to the sides of the base fabric.

5 Using the ½" (1cm) seam allowance, machine-sew all around the edge of the front panel to hold the padded strips in place. Make up the pillow back as shown on page 126 or 127.

tab-top curtain with layered strip detail

This simple design shows how a layering effect can be achieved by using different-width strips of felted wool fabric in two contrasting colors. I have used only two colors to create a sophisticated feel, but it is possible to layer more colors for a different effect. The folds of the fabric emphasize the clean lines of the strip detail, which brings interest whether the curtain is closed or drawn. The layered design runs through the length of the curtain and forms the tab-top heading.

materials + tools

FOR THE MAIN CURTAIN: 52 x 80"
   (130 x 200CM) BLUE FELT OR
   FELTED WOVEN-WOOL FABRIC,
   OR AS REQUIRED FOR THE SIZE
   OF YOUR WINDOW (SEE STEP 1)
FOR THE STRIPS: 80 x 13½" (220 x
   30CM) BLUE FELT OR FELTED
   WOVEN-WOOL FABRIC AND 80 x
   19½" (220 x 48CM) CONTRASTING
   FELT OR FELTED WOVEN-WOOL
   FABRIC FOR THE STRIPS
MATCHING SEWING THREAD
BASIC SEWING KIT
SEWING MACHINE

1 To determine the length of your curtain, measure from the top of the curtain pole to the floor, and subtract 1¾" (4cm) for the drop of the tab-top headings. Measure the width of the window frame and make the curtain one and a half to two times wider to gain the right fullness. Cut a piece of felt fabric to size. Work out how many sets of felt strips you will need for the width of your curtain: the widest strip is 2" (5cm), and the sets are spaced 8" (20cm) apart. You can add strips or adjust the space between strips to suit your needs, but make sure that the first and last strips align with the outer edges of your curtain. This curtain is 52" (130cm) wide and 80" (200cm) long, and there are six sets of layered felt strips.

Cut the sets of felt strips 8" (20cm) longer than the curtain—in this case, 88" (220cm) long. For each set, cut two strips in the contrasting felt—2" (5cm) wide and 1¼" (3cm) wide, and cut two strips in the same fabric as the main curtain—1¾" (4cm) wide and ½" (1cm wide).

opposite Tab tops are among the most basic of curtain headings, but they can be made to look very elegant. Here, the layered strips of felt that create the design detail on the curtain have been formed into loops that function as the tab-top heading.

2 Make up each set of strips in turn, placing one strip centrally on top of another. Start with the widest strip on the bottom and graduate up to the narrowest strip on the top. Pin the layered strips in place.

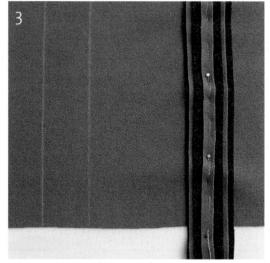

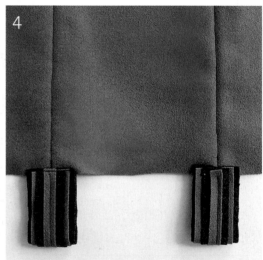

3 Lay the curtain fabric right side up on a large work surface, and use tailor's chalk and a metal ruler to mark guidelines for the felt strips on it. The first 2" (5cm) wide strip is positioned at the left edge of the curtain, with the outer edges of the strip and base fabric aligning, so the first guideline is 2" (5cm) in from the edge. Measure 8" (20cm) from the first guideline and mark the position for the second 2" (5cm) wide strip. Mark the position for the remaining strips in the same way, leaving 8" (20cm) between each one (or whatever measurement you calculated in step 1 in order to ensure that the edge of the last strip aligns with the right edge of the curtain).

Leaving an excess of 8" (20cm) overhanging the top edge of the curtain to make the tab-top heading, tack the layered strips onto the base fabric in the marked positions. Machine-sew the layered strips in place, sewing in a straight line through the center of each one.

4 Lay the curtain wrong side up, and fold back the top of each layered strip to form the tab tops. Overlap the edges by about ½" (1cm), and pin the layered strips to the reverse of the curtain. Check that the curtain is the correct length, and adjust the tab tops if necessary. Machine-sew securely in place to form the loops for the pole.

corrugated-effect storage box

This handy storage box can be used for keeping everything from magazines and newspapers to children's toys neatly in their place. The cardboard inserts in the base and side panels provide a stable structure that holds its shape. The stitching detail on the padded front and back panels is formed using a straightforward quilting technique. The stitching design used for this project creates a corrugated effect that mimics the look of horizontal strips of felt, which could be accentuated even more by using contrasting thread for the stitching.

materials + tools
60 x 26" (150 x 64cm) LIGHT OLIVE FELT OR
    FELTED WOVEN-WOOL FABRIC
21 x 16" (54 x 40cm) OF $^3/_4$"- (2cm-) THICK BATTING
2 PIECES OF STRONG, THICK CARDBOARD TO
    STIFFEN THE SIDES, 8 x 10$^3/_4$" (20 x 27cm)
1 PIECE OF STRONG, THICK CARDBOARD TO
    STIFFEN THE BASE, 8 x 16" (20 x 40cm)
MATCHING SEWING THREAD
BASIC SEWING KIT
SEWING MACHINE

1 Cut a piece of fabric measuring 17 x 60" (42 x 150cm) for the main body of the storage box. Fold the fabric in half, short end to short end, with right sides facing; using a $^1/_2$" (1cm) seam allowance, pin and then machine-sew the ends together. Turn the fabric right side out and lay it flat in front of you with the seam on top. Using a metal ruler and tailor's chalk, draw a line 8" (20cm) from the seam—this section forms the 8" (20cm) wide base of the storage box. Center this section so that there are equal measurements on either side—these 10$^3/_4$" (27cm) wide sections form the front and back panels of the storage box. Pin the two layers of fabric together, then machine-sew along the seam and the marked line to form three "pockets"—the base of the box and the front and back panels.

2 Using a metal ruler and tailor's chalk, draw six parallel lines ³⁄₈" (1cm) apart on both the front and back panels of the storage box, starting at the bottom and working your way up. Leave a gap of 4³⁄₈" (10cm), then draw another 11 parallel lines, again spacing them ³⁄₈" (1cm) apart.

Cut two pieces of batting slightly narrower than the front and back panels of the storage box—these will be approximately 16 x 10¼" (40 x 26cm). Insert the two pieces of batting into the "pockets" of the front and back panels.

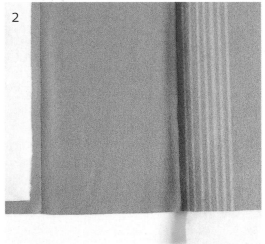 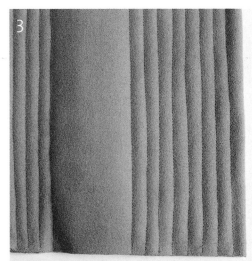

3 Make sure that the batting is completely hidden within the "pockets" and that it is smooth and flat, then hold the layers of fabric in place with a few pins so that they don't move around when you are sewing.

Using either matching or contrasting thread, depending on the effect you wish to create, machine-sew along all the marked lines on the front and back panels of the storage box to create the corrugated "strips" effect. Make sure that your lines of stitching are completely straight.

4 To make the sides of the box, first cut handles in the cardboard inserts. These measure 1¾ x 4" (4 x 10cm) and are positioned 2" (5cm) down from the top edge and 2" (5cm) in from each side. Cut two pieces of fabric measuring 9 x 23" (22 x 58cm). Fold one piece of fabric in half around one of the cardboard inserts, with the fold of the fabric at the top of the insert and the join at the bottom.

5 Using an equal ½" (1cm) seam allowance on both sides, pin the two layers of fabric together along the bottom and sides. Machine-sew closely around using a zipper foot, enclosing the cardboard. Repeat to make the other side panel.

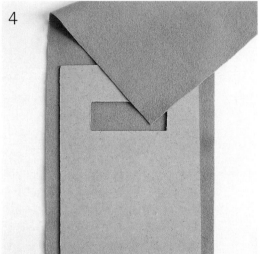

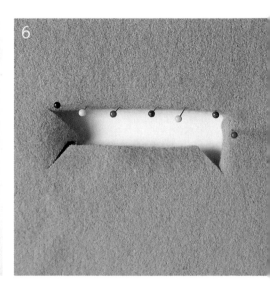

6 Taking one of the side panels, feel where the center point of each handle is through the fabric; cut through both layers of fabric at this point. Leaving a sufficient hem allowance to tuck under around the inside of the handle, carefully cut diagonally into the fabric at each corner. Fold the fabric under to hide the raw edges, and pin along the inside of the handle, then neatly hand-stitch to hold in place. Repeat the process to create the other handle in the second side panel.

opposite The felt storage box offers a soft solution for all your storage needs, bringing warmth, texture, and color into your interior. The parallel lines of stitching, shown here with matching thread, imitate the effect of strips of felt.

7 To strengthen the base of the storage box, insert the remaining piece of cardboard into the bottom "pocket." Slide it between the layers of fabric until there is ½" (1cm) clear at each end for the seam allowance.

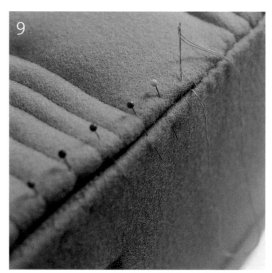

8 Attach the side panels to the base of the storage box. With right sides together, align the bottom seam of the side panel with the ½" (1cm) seam allowance at one end of the base panel. Machine-sew the two panels together, sewing along the stitch line at the bottom of the side panel. Repeat to attach the other side panel to the other end of the base panel.

9 Turn the structure over so right sides are facing out as you assemble the storage box. Lift up the sides and front and back panels, and pin the edges together, folding the seam allowance to the inside. Neatly hand-stitch in place.

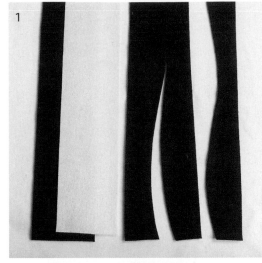

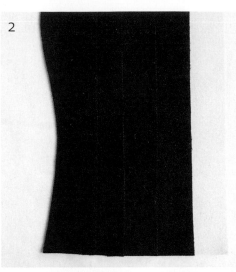

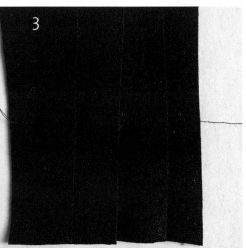

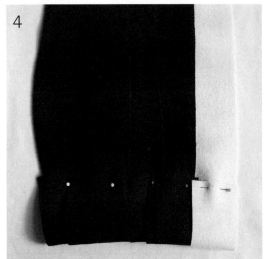

materials + tools

48 x 32" (120 x 80CM) BRIGHT
RED FELT OR FELTED WOVEN-
WOOL FABRIC

16 x 32" (40 x 80CM) CREAM FELT
OR FELTED WOVEN-WOOL FABRIC

2 METAL OR WOODEN DOWELS,
APPROXIMATELY $^5/_8$" (1.5CM)
DIAMETER AND 43" (110CM) LONG

MATCHING SEWING THREAD

BASIC SEWING KIT

SEWING MACHINE

1 Cut the red and cream felt into strips measuring 4 x 32" (10 x 80cm). Next, cut down the center of each strip in an irregular wavy line, to form two strips approximately 2" (5cm) wide, each with one straight and one wavy edge.

2 Start laying the strips out on a large work surface, wrong side up, overlapping them by approximately $^3/_4$" (2cm) so that the wavy edge is visible on the right side of the wall hanging. Alternate the colors randomly, as you wish.

3 When you are happy with the arrangement, check that your wall hanging is the correct width

for the poles, and add or take away strips as necessary. Pin, then tack the strips of felt together 4" (10cm) from the top and bottom edges. Using straight stitch and matching thread, machine-sew the strips together along the line of tacking.

4 To form casings for the poles, fold the ends of the strips toward the back along the top and bottom edges of the wall hanging, and pin them in place along your previous lines of stitching.

5 Machine-sew in place, following the existing stitch lines. Insert the poles through the casings, and hang the finished wall hanging.

wavy strips
wall hanging

The inspiration for this wall hanging
was the continual rippling effect of
moving water. Two different colors of felt
have been cut into strips with one wavy
edge, and sewn together side by side,
ovelapping each other in places. Different
effects can be created by experimenting
with the spacing between the strips,
especially as the layered sections can look
very different depending on the lighting.
The balance between the colors can also
be varied according to your décor. Here,
the vibrant red and cream felt create a
dramatic effect in this minimal interior.

ottoman with **spiral detail**

This bright yellow cylindrical ottoman brings a splash of sunshine inside. A layer of batting between the foam insert and the felt that makes up the sliced spiral surface detail adds fullness to the top of the ottoman and helps to accentuate the three-dimensional aspect of the design. The circular top piece of the ottoman is attached to the sides with a visible external seam, which is in keeping with the spiral design and helps to unify the piece.

previous spread The graphic sliced spiral design would also work well for a circular pillow cover—you could make one to tie in with the ottoman, reversing the contrasting colors by using cream on the outside with yellow underneath .

materials + tools
MEDIUM-HARD FOAM CYLINDER, 8" (20CM) HIGH,
 24" (60CM) DIAMETER
TWO 26 x 26" (65 x 65CM) PIECES OF YELLOW FELT
 OR FELTED WOVEN-WOOL FABRIC
 (FOR THE TOP AND BOTTOM)
TWO 9 x 39" (23 x 98CM) STRIPS OF YELLOW FELT
 OR FELTED WOVEN-WOOL FABRIC (FOR THE SIDES)
26 x 26" (65 x 65CM) CREAM FELT OR FELTED
 WOVEN-WOOL FABRIC
26 x 26" (65 x 65CM) OF $^3/_4$"- (2CM-) THICK
 POLYESTER BATTING
26 x 26" (65 x 65CM) PLAIN COTTON FABRIC
CREAM SEWING THREAD
BASIC SEWING KIT
SEWING MACHINE

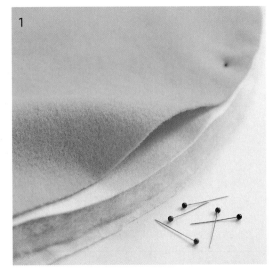

1 Cut two circles of yellow felt measuring 25" (63cm) in diameter. Cut three more circles of the same size, one in cream felt, one in cotton, and one in batting. Cut two strips of yellow felt measuring 9 x 39" (23 x 98cm) for the sides of the ottoman.

 Put a yellow circle to one side for the base of the ottoman, then layer the remaining circles on top of each other, starting with the cotton at the bottom, then the batting, then the cream felt, and ending with the yellow felt on top. Pin the layers together.

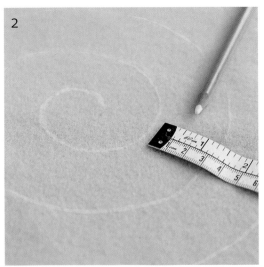

2 Using tailor's chalk and starting in the middle of the yellow felt circle (12$^1/_2$"/31.5cm from the edge), draw a spiral outward, leaving 1$^3/_4$" (4cm) between each consecutive circle. Continue drawing the spiral all the way to the outer edge of the circle, trailing off when you reach the edge.

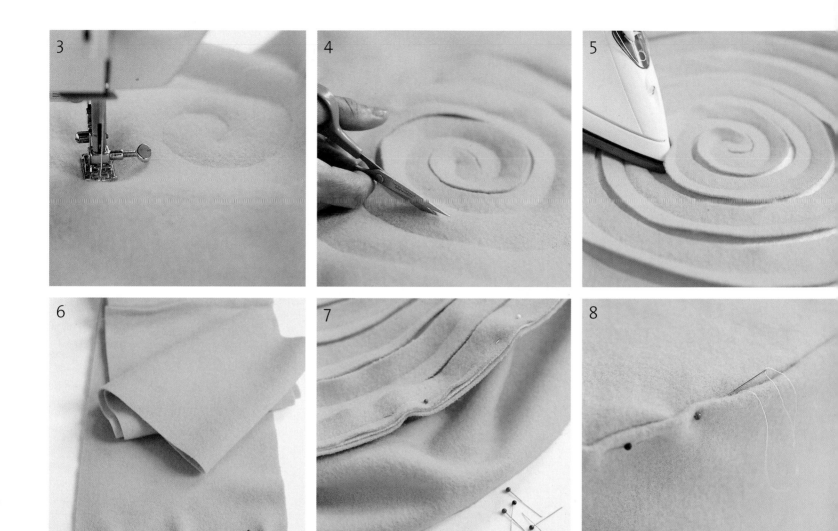

3 Using cream thread and starting in the center of the circle, machine-sew along the marked spiral, working your way outward to the edge of the circle. When turning the layers of fabric as you sew, remember to push down firmly, in order to ensure that the layers stay in position.

4 Using sharp, pointed scissors and starting in the center, cut through the top layer of yellow felt only, snipping halfway between the stitch lines. Continue until you reach the edge of the circle.

5 Using a hot iron, steam-press the cut edges of the spiral upward, to give them more height.

6 For the side panel, join the two strips of felt end to end to form a ring. To do this, pin, then machine-sew, the short edges with right sides together, using a ½" (1.5cm) seam allowance.

7 Trim the excess batting and cotton from the edge of the layered circle. With right sides facing out and the seam on the outside, pin the edge of the layered circle to the top edge of the side panel, then machine-sew ½" (1.5cm) from the edge.

8 Place the cover over the foam insert. Pin, then hand-stitch, the felt base to the bottom of the side panel, turning in the ½" (1.5cm) seam allowance.

throw with **contrasting strips**

The long stitched strip detail in black and white is designed to break up the surface of this bright blue throw. This effect is achieved by slicing into the blue throw and sewing layered black and white strips between each section to raise the seam above the blue background and make it a design feature. The throw is reversible, with a different effect on the side where the stitching is not visible. You can add more rows of layered strips if you wish, spacing them at regular intervals across the throw, or just break up part of the background fabric as I have here. And of course, the strips can be made in any accent color you desire.

materials + tools
51 x 60" (128 x 150CM) BRIGHT BLUE FELT
    OR FELTED WOVEN-WOOL FABRIC
2¼ x 60" (6 x 150CM) BLACK FELT OR
    FELTED WOVEN-WOOL FABRIC
4½ x 60" (12 x 150CM) WHITE FELT OR
    FELTED WOVEN-WOOL FABRIC
MATCHING SEWING THREAD
BASIC SEWING KIT
SEWING MACHINE

1 Cut the main bright blue background fabric into four sections, one measuring 10½ x 60" (26 x 150cm), two measuring 6 x 60" (15 x 150cm), and one measuring 28½ x 60" (72 x 150cm).

For the detail, cut three strips of black felt measuring ¾ x 60" (2 x 150cm) and six strips of white felt measuring ¾ x 60" (2 x 150cm).

opposite This technique provides another great way to use up narrow scraps of fabric. You can make the layered strips as colorful as you like, or take a more understated approach by using only three contrasting colors, as I have here. As well as brightening up a sofa, this design would work well as a bedspread.

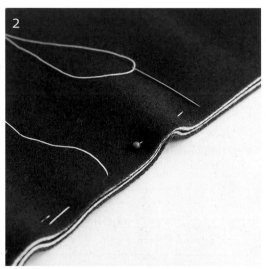

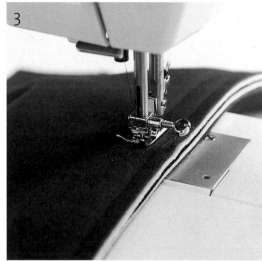

2 On a large flat work surface, lay one strip of black felt between two strips of white felt. Sandwich the pile of strips between the edges of the 28½"- (72cm-) wide section and one of the 6"- (15cm-) wide sections of the main bright blue fabric. Align the edges neatly, and pin and then tack the layers of fabric together.

3 Using matching thread and straight stitch, machine-sew the seam ¼" (5mm) in from the edge. Remove the tacking, and machine-sew another parallel line ½" (1cm) in from the first.

Repeat for the other two sets of contrasting strips, layering the second set as before and sandwiching it between the two 6"- (15cm-) wide sections of the main bright blue throw. Pin, tack, and machine-sew in place with two parallel lines of straight stitch, as before. Layer the third set of strips, and join the remaining 10½"- (26cm-) wide sections of the throw in the same way.

basics

sewing terms

hand-stitching

❋ **tacking or basting** Use this technique to hold pieces of fabric together before machine-sewing. Tacking makes the fabric lie flatter than pinning, producing a neater finish. It is also easier to sew over. use contrasting thread that shows up well on your chosen fabric, and sew long stitches, so that the thread can be easily removed after machine-sewing.

❋ **gathering stitches** Use very strong polyester thread when working on the gathered projects, as it is less likely to break when you pull the thread to gather up the fabric, and it will also help to prevent the ruched folds from unraveling before they are machine-sewn in place.

❋ **invisible stitch** Use when closing a seam, or a gap in a seam, with hand-stitching. Use small neat stitches, slipping the thread through opposite folds of fabric for about $\frac{1}{4}$" (5mm) before bringing the needle out and drawing the thread through.

machine-sewing

❋ **sewing machine needles** When working with heavy materials like felt and felted woven-wool fabric, use strong needles, such as those intended for sewing tough fabrics like denim or leather (sizes 90–100 are ideal).

❋ **thread** Use strong cotton, polycotton, or polyester threads to sew felt, and make sure that you use the same quality threads on the sewing machine and the bobbin to ensure the correct tension.

❋ **running stitch** Unless otherwise specified, use a small to medium length straight stitch for the projects in this book. Practice on a scrap of fabric first, to ensure that the tension is correct.

tip

❋ **maintenance** Clean your sewing machine regularly, as the wool fibers can build up over time and may cause it to jam.

basic sewing kit

1 **fabric tape measure** A flexible ruler is handy for measuring fabric, as well as curved surfaces such as the circumference of a lampshade, round pillow, or ottoman. A tape measure with both imperial and metric measurements can be useful, but always stick to one set of measurements within each project for consistency.

2 **needles** A selection of needles is essential for hand-sewing. When working with felt and felted woven-wool fabric, use a medium-sized needle with a sharp point for general sewing. Use a long needle for sewing gathering stitches. A large eye will make threading the needle easier.

3 **metal ruler** Use for measuring and drawing straight lines. A metal ruler is essential for projects where you need to mark out pleats or guidelines.

4 **fabric marker** Markers are available in the form of a pen, pencil, or traditional tailor's chalk. A special white textile marker will show up well on most colors of felt. The pencil or chalk marks will rub off easily, while the pen is designed to fade over time.

5 **pins** Essential for holding fabric in place before sewing, pins should be strong enough and long enough to accommodate thick felt (0.65mm thick and $1\frac{1}{2}$"/38mm long should be adequate). Pins with plastic or glass heads are easier to push through thick material. Safety pins are also useful to have in your sewing kit, for threading drawstrings through casings.

6 **small scissors** Used for trimming loose threads, small scissors with a sharp point are more accurate for cutting out small shapes, and essential for cutout projects such as the Table Runner and Place Mats (see pages 74–79).

7 **large scissors** Use large, sharp dressmaker's scissors for cutting out larger pieces of fabric. Avoid cutting paper or cardboard with your fabric scissors, as this will blunt them.

sewn-in pillow back

This is a really easy and quick way to apply a pillow backing, and requires only a small amount of hand-sewing. The back panel of the pillow is cut in one piece, to the same size as the front panel. The front and back panels are pinned together, with right sides facing, then machine-sewn along three sides using a ½" (1cm) seam allowance. Once the cover has been turned right side out and the pillow form inserted, the seam is turned in along the fourth side and closed with invisible stitching. The drawback to this method is that, once sew in, the pillow cover cannot be easily removed for washing, and would require picking out the seam and resewing.

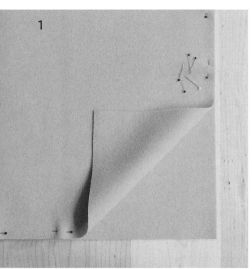

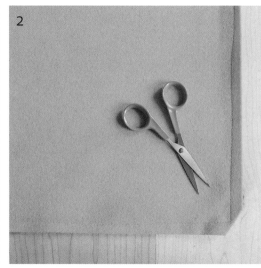

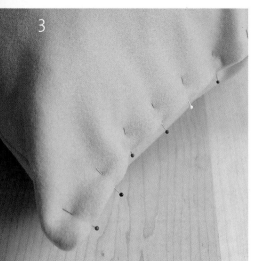

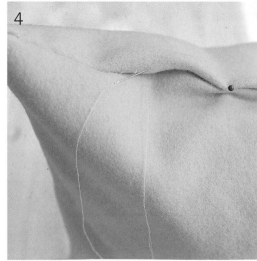

1 Cut a piece of fabric for the back of the pillow cover to the same size as the front panel, including the same ½" (1cm) seam allowance (or as specified). Place the two panels with right sides together, and pin along the seam allowance on three sides, leaving the fourth side open.

2 Using matching thread and a small to medium sized straight stitch, machine-sew along the three sides to join the front and back panels together, removing the pins as you sew. Cut off the corners on the diagonal, being careful not to cut through the stitching—this will produce neater corners on the finished pillow.

3 Turn the pillow cover right side out and insert the pillow form. To close the fourth side of the cover, fold the ½" (1cm) seam allowance to the inside and pin the edges together.

4 Stitch the two sides together, keeping the stitches as invisible as possible. To do this, work from right to left if you are right-handed and from left to right (as shown) if you are left-handed. Knot the end of the thread, and bring the needle and thread out through one folded edge. Slip the needle through the fold of the opposite edge for about ¼" (5mm); bring the needle out and draw the thread through. Continue to slip the needle and thread through the opposing folded edges.

pillow back **with zipper**

Although sewing in a zipper requires a degree of technical skill, this is still not a complicated way to make up the back of a pillow cover, and it is the method that I would recommend using, as it does mean that the cover can be easily removed for cleaning. The back panel of the pillow cover is cut in two pieces, which are joined together in the middle by the zipper, running horizontally. You will need a metal or nylon closed-end zipper in a color that matches your pillow cover. The zipper should be the same length as the pillow form.

1 Cut two pieces of fabric for the back cover. Both should be the same width as the front cover (adding a ½" (1cm) side-seam allowance, or as specified); one should be 1½" (3cm) longer than half the length of the front cover, and the other should be 1" (2cm) longer, giving a ½" (1cm) seam allowance along the top and bottom edges, and a 1" (2cm) and ½" (1cm) seam allowance along the inner zip edges respectively. With the fabric wrong side up, fold in 1" (2cm) along the inner edge of the larger back piece, and press.

2 With the zipper wrong side up, pin one side of the zipper tape along the cut edge of the fold, with ½" (1cm) clear at each end for the side seams. Open the zipper. Using the zipper foot, machine-sew the tape in place along the folded edge.

3 Pin the other side of the zipper tape along the inner edge of the other back piece, with the fabric right side up. Machine-sew in place.

4 Fold the edge over to form a neat fold aligning with the zipper's teeth. Machine-sew in place.

5 With the zipper half open, pin the front and back covers with right sides together. Using a ½" (1cm) seam allowance, machine-sew around the edges. Cut the corners (shown in step 2 opposite); turn right side out, and insert the pillow form.

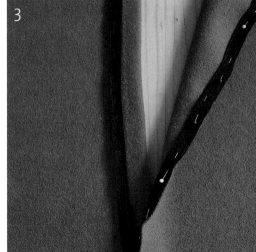

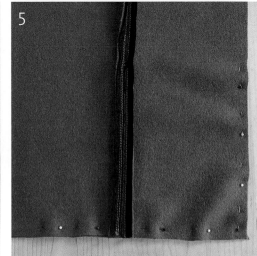

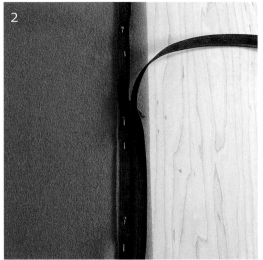

opposite Think creatively, and you may come up with new ways to make a decorative feature out of your stitching. Here, the machine-sewing that holds the appliqué circles in place becomes integral to the design of the pillow—the "scribble" effect means that you don't need to be too neat, either (see pages 80–83). Think about the result you are trying to achieve. In some cases, using thread in a contrasting color is all that is needed to create a completely different look.

this page Batting is another material that can be used to alter the finished look of many of the projects in the book, in particular to create or enhance a three-dimensional effect. It is used here, under the top layer of felt on the ottoman, to bring out the texture of the spiral design (see pages 114–117). It is also used to pad the appliqué circles and create a "bubble" effect on the pillow shown opposite. Without it, the appliqué design would be flat.

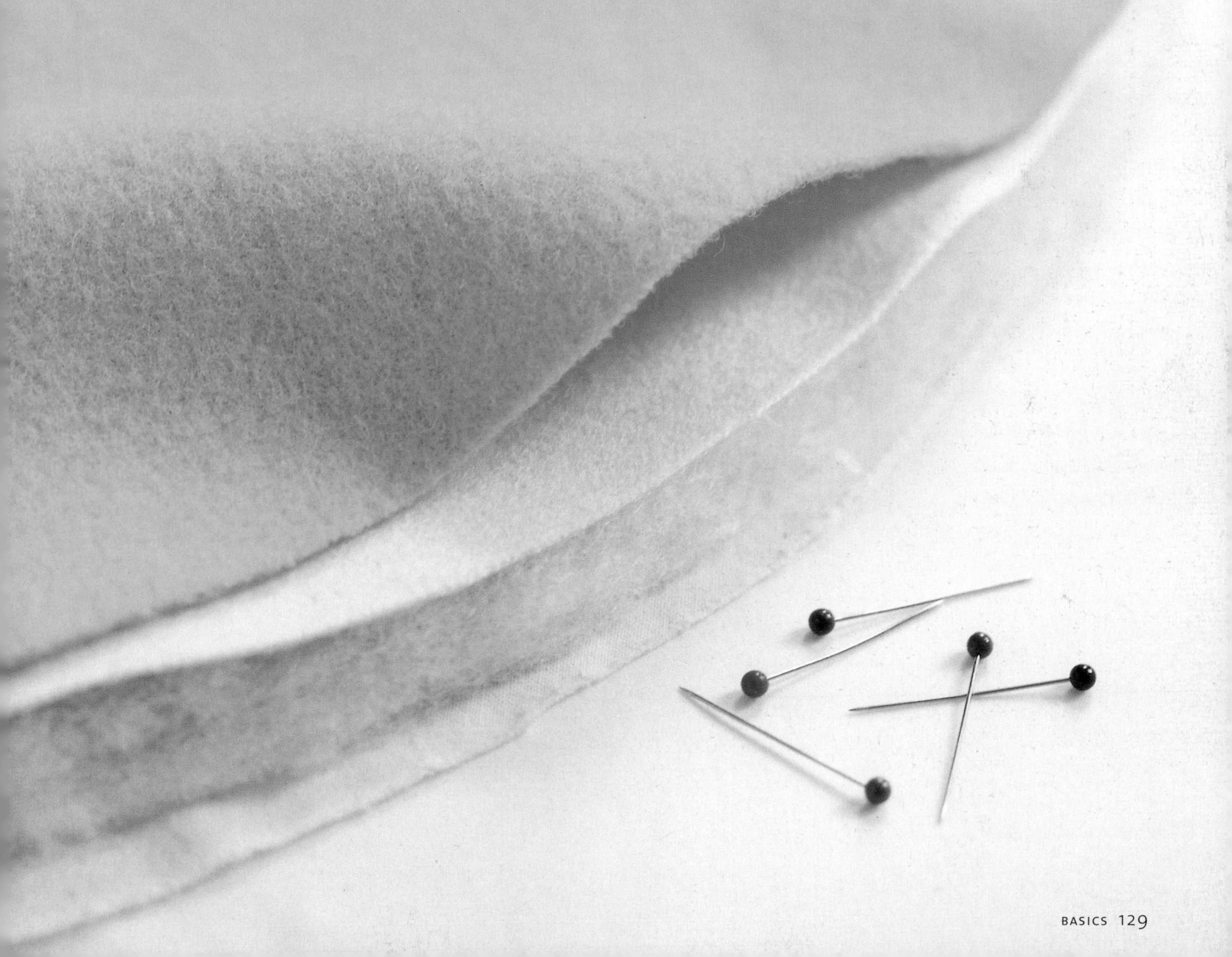

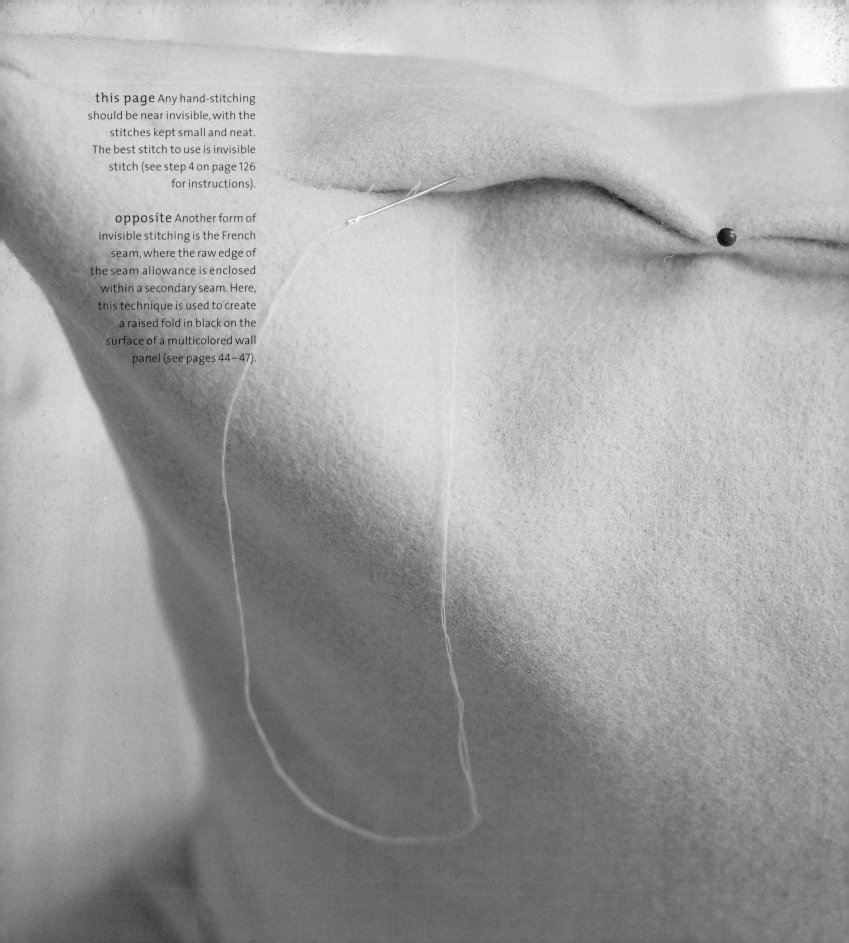

this page Any hand-stitching should be near invisible, with the stitches kept small and neat. The best stitch to use is invisible stitch (see step 4 on page 126 for instructions).

opposite Another form of invisible stitching is the French seam, where the raw edge of the seam allowance is enclosed within a secondary seam. Here, this technique is used to create a raised fold in black on the surface of a multicolored wall panel (see pages 44–47).

easy folded felt details

Trimmings are a great way to add color and interest to soft furnishings. These quick-to-make felt embellishments can be applied to anything from pillows and lampshades to slippers and scarves. The flower shapes could also be worn as corsages—simply use a brooch back or safety pin to attach them to your lapel. You only need small pieces of felt to make these decorations, so they are a great way to use up leftover scraps. It is fun to play around with felt, folding, pleating, or gathering it, and seeing what new shapes and adornments you can come up with.

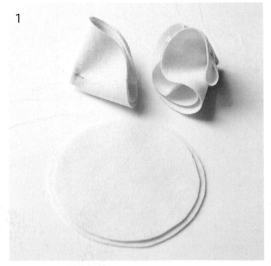

materials + tools

SCRAPS OF FELT OR FELTED WOVEN-WOOL FABRIC
IN DIFFERENT COLORS
MATCHING SEWING THREAD
BASIC SEWING KIT
SEWING MACHINE

1 Cut two circles of cream felt, one slightly smaller than the other—approximately $2\,{}^{3}\!/\!{}_{4}$" (7cm) and 3" (8cm) in diameter. Center the smaller circle on top of the larger one. Fold them into a semicircle, and then into a quarter. Hand-stitch through the corner to hold the folds in place at the base. Open out the felt form to create a flower shape.

opposite Decorative felt details can be used to embellish anything from pillows to clothes. Here, fresh lime-green flowers add a bright touch to charcoal-gray felt slippers (see pages 136–137). Simply position the flower on the top part of the slipper, then stitch through the base to secure in place.

2 Cut a strip of red felt ½" (1cm) wide and 20" (50cm) long. Starting at one end, fold the strip into random-sized loops, creating irregular shapes. Pinch the form in the middle and secure with a pin as you work. When you are happy with the shape of the loops you have created, hand-stitch through the center to hold them together.

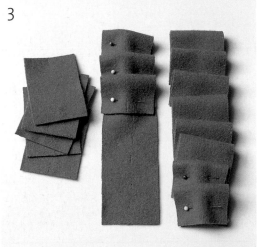

3 Cut a strip of blue felt 2" (5cm) wide and 8" (20cm) long. Cut ten 2 x 2" (5 x 5cm) squares of matching blue felt. Fold the squares in half, and pin them onto the base fabric. Start at the top of the strip, and overlap the cut edge with the folded edge of the first square. Fold the next square in half, and pin it onto the base fabric with the fold to the top, overlapping the pinned square above by half. Repeat until the base fabric is completely covered with folded squares. Using matching thread and straight stitch, machine-sew each folded square in place, holding back the fold of the square below as you sew each one, so that the stitching is hidden from view.

4 Cut a strip of green felt ¾" (2cm) wide and 20" (50cm) long. Starting at one end, fold the strip up into even-sized loops, pinching the form in the middle and securing with a pin as you work. Continue looping the strip back and forth, keeping the size of the loops equal to create a regular shape. Hand-stitch the strips together through the middle.

cozy slippers

These felt slippers are really easy to make and so cozy to wear around the house that I couldn't resist including them here. The shape is very basic, so it is not difficult to resize the template as necessary. Either keep your slippers unadorned, or embellish them by applying a decorative felt detail of your choice, made by folding or pleating pieces of felt in different ways (see pages 132–135). These embellishments can help to create a more feminine look, and can be made in the same color or a contrasting shade, depending on the effect you like.

left Felt slippers are very warm and comfortable to wear. These examples, in chic dark gray, are so presentable that they don't need to be confined to bedtime, but can be worn around the house at any time of day.

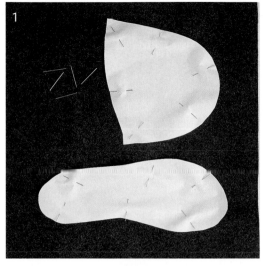

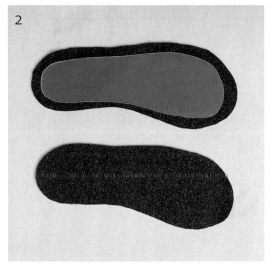

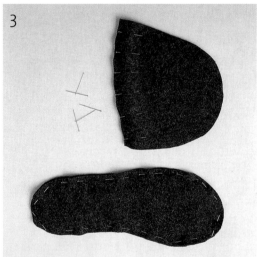

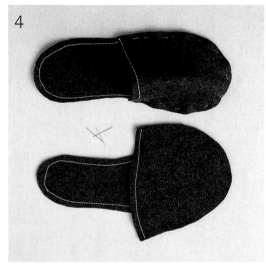

materials + tools

20 x 24" (50 x 60cm) THICK
    DARK GRAY FELT OR FELTED
    WOVEN-WOOL FABRIC
THIN CARDBOARD OR FLEXIBLE PLASTIC
    SHEET TO MAKE THE TEMPLATE
16 x 16" (40 x 40cm) OF
    POLYPROPYLENE PLASTIC,
    OR ANY HARD FLEXIBLE PLASTIC
    FOR THE INSERTS
MATCHING SEWING THREAD
BASIC SEWING KIT
SEWING MACHINE

1 Fold the felt in half and, using the templates on page 141, cut out two fabric bases and two top pieces for each foot. Cut one plastic insert for each base, ½" (1cm) smaller than the fabric bases.

2 For each foot, place the plastic insert between the two fabric bases, aligning the edges of the fabric and making sure that the plastic insert is positioned centrally.

3 Pin the edges of the two fabric bases together with the plastic in the middle, pinning as close to the plastic as possible to keep it tight within the fabric. Pin the two top pieces together along the bottom curve only, aligning the edges neatly. Using matching thread (we used contrasting thread so that it shows up clearly), machine-sew around the base of the slipper, following the pins and removing them as you sew; then stitch along the bottom curve of the top piece, sewing ¼" (5mm) in from the edge.

4 Pin the top part of the slipper to the base, with the longer side on the outer side of the slipper. The rounded shape means that you will need to ease it into place to create a neat slipper shape. Machine-sew together, keeping in line with the stitch line on the base of the slipper.

table runner + place mats
with **cutout shapes**
PAGES 74–79

This template is shown at 100 percent. Trace onto thin
cardboard or a flexible plastic sheet and cut out.

pinched-petal lampshade

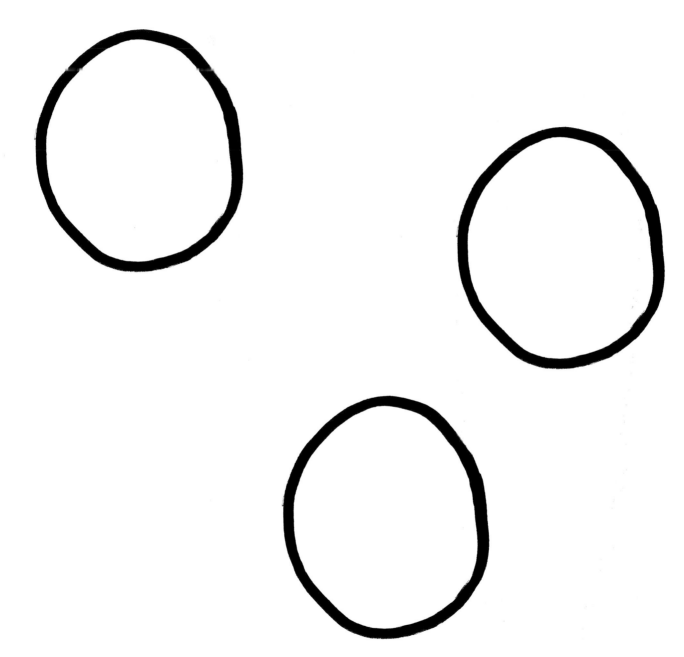

These "petal" templates are shown at 100 percent. Trace onto thin cardboard or a flexible plastic sheet and cut out.

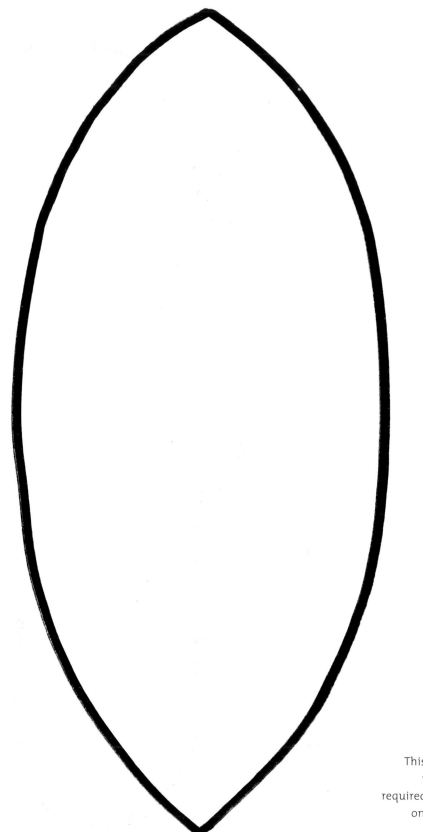

This template is shown at 85 percent. The original template measures 10" (25 cm) long and 4" (11 cm) wide. Resize as required on a photocopier. Trace the template at the correct size onto thin cardboard or a flexible plastic sheet and cut out.

TEMPLATE
cozy slippers
PAGES 135–137

These templates are shown at 100 percent and are size Medium. Draw around your left foot on a piece of paper and measure the length of the outline from heel to toe. Using a photocopier, enlarge the template for the sole of the slipper to the size of your foot, adding a ½" (1cm) seam allowance all around. Enlarge the template for the top of the slipper by the same amount. Trace the template at the correct size onto thin cardboard or a flexible plastic sheet and cut out. When cutting out the right foot, turn the template over and use the reverse.

resources

for felt:

AETNA FELT CORPORATION
Aetnafelt.com
2401 W. Emaus Avenue
Allentown, PA 18103
800-526-4451

A CHILD'S DREAM COME TRUE
Achildsdream.com
1223-D Michigan Street
Sandpoint, ID 83864
800-359-2906

DENVER FABRICS
Denverfabrics.com
800-468-0602

DICK BLICK ART MATERIALS
Dickblick.com
Nationwide locations
800-933-2542

DISTINCTIVE FABRIC
Distinctivefabric.com
877-721-7269

FABRIC.COM
888-455-2940

FELTORAMA.COM
888-393-4050

THE FELT PEOPLE
Thefeltpeople.com
800-631-8968

HANCOCK FABRICS
Hancockfabrics.com
877-322-9427

J. CAROLINE CREATIVE
Jcarolinecreative.com
866-522-7654

JO-ANN FABRIC AND CRAFT STORES
(also sells pillow forms and notions)
Joann.com
Nationwide locations
888-739-4120

JOGGLES.COM
401-615-7696
One Stitch at a Time
Onestitchatatime.com
609-397-4545
Onlinefabricstore.net
(also sells pillow forms)

PEARL
Pearlpaint.com
800-451-7327

PRAIRIE POINT JUNCTION QUILT SHOP
Woolfeltcentral.com
124 East 8th/P.O. Box 184
Cozad, Nebraska 69130
308-784-2010

TRIM FABRIC
Trimfabric.com

VINTAGE VOGUE
Vintagevogue.com
712 June Drive
Corona, CA 92879
951-279-9115

for pillow forms:

MICHAEL'S
(also sells notions)
Michaels.com
Nationwide locations
800-MICHAELS

PILLOWSXPRESS.COM
877-3-PILLOW

SOFTSHAPESDIRECT.COM
800-338-4776

for sewing notions:

A.C. MOORE
ACMoore.com
Nationwide locations
888-ACMOORE

NANCY'S NOTIONS
Nancysnotions.com
800-833-0690

STEINLAUF AND STOLLER INC.
steinlaufandstoller.com
239 West 39th Street
New York, NY 10018
877-869-0321

acknowledgments

I would like to thank everyone who worked incredibly hard under pressure to make this book happen.

In particular, I would like to thank my husband, Gavin, for providing me with support and help, without which this book would not have been possible.

I would like to thank my team, who worked very hard on all the projects and steps, especially: Rachel Jones, Lucy Gaughan, Elizabeth Sellers, Luzelle van der Westhuizen, and Emma Long.

I wish to thank Chris Everard for his superb photography, and Zia Mattocks and Valerie Fong for helping to keep everything on track.

I would also like to thank the people who kindly let us use their homes as locations for photography.

the publisher

would like to thank Andrew Weaving, of Century, for the kind loan of furniture for the photo shoot for this book.

Century
58 Blandford Street
London W1U 7JB
Tel: +44 (0)20 7487 5100
www.centuryd.com
shop@centuryd.com